MASTERING MY MISTAKES
IN THE KITCHEN

MASTERING MY MISTAKES IN THE KITCHEN

LEARNING TO COOK

WITH

65 GREAT CHEFS

AND OVER

100 DELICIOUS RECIPES

DANA COWIN

WITH JULIA TURSHEN

ecco

An Imprint of HarperCollinsPublishers

HarperCollins books may be purchased for educational, business, or sales promotional use. For information please e-mail the Special Markets Department @ SPsales@harpercollins.com.

FIRST EDITION

Book design by Suet Yee Chong
Concept design by Patricia Sanchez

Library of Congress Cataloging-in-Publication Data has been applied for.

ISBN 978-0-06-230590-9

14 15 16 17 18   IND/QGT   10 9 8 7 6 5 4 3 2 1

To my mother,
who believed my mistakes
were "learning experiences,"
and
to my father,
who seemed to believe
I never made any mistakes at all

contents

FOREWORD

Julia Child said, in *My Life in France*, "One of the secrets, and pleasures, of cooking is to learn to correct something if it goes awry; and one of the lessons is to grin and bear it if it cannot be fixed." Julia also spoke about never admitting to a mistake because most people will never know you made one. This is certainly true, and it's something that cooks do often. But learning from our mistakes is one of the most important things to do, in and out of the kitchen. If we have made mistakes, it is often because we have pushed ourselves. As cooks, we learn not only to accept the mistakes we make, but understand what we can learn from them. And we learn not to make that mistake again.

Dana Cowin's *Mastering My Mistakes in the Kitchen* takes Julia Child's credo to heart. A self-taught and determined cook, Dana documents what she has learned from her mistakes. There to guide her is a cadre of fine chefs with whom Dana has forged friendships as they have graced the pages of *Food & Wine* over the years.

As the chefs help Dana right her wrongs, she gives us a unique insider's view into common challenges that we all have faced in the kitchen. Jacques Pépin demystifies the intimidating soufflé with his no-fail secret and waxes poetic on the importance of timing and even-temperature baking. Daniel Holzman shows Dana the trick to making light and tender meatballs and testing for doneness. Andrew Zimmern walks Dana through a chicken stir-fry with peanuts, revealing the power of celery and how to embrace cornstarch. I also weigh in with my three-step, foolproof technique for wonderful roasted chicken.

The concept of *mise en place*—French for "put in place"—is essential to the high-functioning kitchen. More than the organizing of tools and ingredients at one's station, mise en place is a mental state, one of being fully prepared. Through each chapter of her book, Dana gathers her mise en place, experiencing firsthand the importance of organization and ingredients, and as you read, you can see how each lesson she's had has become ingrained in the way she cooks and the way she lives, and you learn along with her.

In the kitchen, as in life, nothing educates us quite like our own errors. You can think of it as learning the hard way. But if everything were perfect, how would we progress? What we can take away from Dana's journey is that you shouldn't just do what you are good at, avoiding things that are harder or take work. As you read, you'll find yourself motivated to take joy and pleasure in working on something to get better. That said, each of the recipes Dana takes on is meant to be doable. If you make a mistake, don't automatically blame the book! Like Dana, take responsibility for your mistake, learn from it and move forward. In doing so, you'll encounter some of the many life lessons disguised in this kitchen education.

When I meet young or new cooks looking for guidance, I offer them two words. The first word is *patience*. I remind anyone starting out on an ambitious task to take time to learn the skills they will need. Do not rush! Cooking is fun, it is rewarding and it gives us the opportunity to nurture others. That is the real reason we cook. Be patient and enjoy where you are while you are there.

The second word is *persistence*. Don't let anyone tell you you can't do something. Try, try, try! I became who I am today because I believed in myself. I never gave up, I couldn't and wouldn't.

These words resonate for me as I read the advice great chefs have given Dana. Throughout her recipes, Dana practices great patience and persistence, never giving up and measuring her ambition with what she has learned from the past. It takes courage to do what Dana has done with *Mastering My Mistakes in the Kitchen*, pushing herself out of her comfort zone and continuing to experience new things, to grow and evolve. In her personal journey, Dana shows us that these qualities are what make us successful, in and out of the kitchen.

Dana already has found success in elevating how we think about food in *Food & Wine*. When we think about food and wine, these two iconic symbols that bring great pleasure to us and the people around us, we don't always look behind the scenes at the journey that made this joy possible. In *Mastering My Mistakes in the Kitchen*, Dana takes us on that journey.

—THOMAS KELLER
CHEF/PROPRIETOR,
THOMAS KELLER RESTAURANT GROUP

INTRODUCTION

I am going to be honest: I am not a great cook.

As the longtime editor-in-chief of *Food & Wine* magazine, I've learned a lot about food by eating in extraordinary restaurants, tasting recipes in our test kitchen daily and talking to chefs. Yet, despite all that, there's one culinary area in which I am not an expert: actual hands-on cooking.

I've messed up literally every type of food (meat, fish, chicken, bread, pie), using every kind of technique (roasting, grilling, broiling, boiling) at every time of day (breakfast, lunch, dinner, snack). And I'm always surprised by my mistakes—particularly because, by the standards of today's foodies, I'm not an adventurous cook. I gravitate toward straightforward recipes with a high "yum" factor, a shortish ingredient list and a smart, simple trick that makes the dish seem special.

I come by my incompetence genetically. I am descended from a long line of noncooks. My mother goes out for dinner or cocktails seven nights a week. She does serve one family meal a year at home: she hosts our annual Thanksgiving feast. To the best of my knowledge, though, she has never considered cooking it herself. She has it delivered by a (very good) local takeout shop and instead devotes her time to whimsical touches like finding colorful paper turkeys and writing our names on them for place cards or procuring a selection of extraordinary desserts.

I wasn't one of those kids who compensated for their parents' lack of interest in food preparation by learning to cook for myself. My friend Caroline from grade school remembers the time when we were eleven and I burned the Formica countertop in the kitchen by putting a hot pan of popcorn directly on it. The incident is seared in my memory, but apparently I had forgotten one small detail: I asked Caroline to tell my parents that she was the one who scorched the counter to avoid getting in trouble. My friend Adina recalls a time just after college when we were peeling apples side by side. I marveled at her ability to remove the peel all in one go: my apples were a patchwork of hack marks, bald spots and red skin. I wasn't a natural.

Once I got to *Food & Wine* in my mid-thirties, I did begin experimenting in the kitchen. On occasional Saturday nights, I'd make dinner for friends, hoping one of them might bring an eligible single guy along. In the office the next week, I'd share my party disasters with the test kitchen cooks and Tina Ujlaki, the executive food editor. They were always gracious and encouraging, offering advice, easier recipes, suggestions for equipment that would make any dish foolproof. They insisted the mistakes weren't my fault. I wasn't so sure. Tina and I created a column for the magazine in which I recounted my kitchen mistakes and she fixed them. At the time, though, I was too embarrassed to let the world know about all my failures, from lumpy crepes to hopeless beef stews. So I used a pseudonym, Irma—a little inside joke referring to Irma Rombauer, who wrote the seminal *Joy of Cooking*. I loved the idea of the real Irma needing help in the kitchen.

But over time, something changed. I figured out how to make certain recipes without failing—some involved nothing more than chopping, tossing and assembling. Those successes were very satisfying, and I've shared many of them in this book. I also realized it was more important to me to come clean about my failures and address my incompetence than it was to hide my inadequacy. Good cooking starts with honesty.

And so began my journey to master my mistakes and to become a better cook. Who better to teach me than the talented chefs whose restaurant meals have been an education in themselves? So I asked some of my chef friends to help me with my favorite recipes, the ones I've made for family and friends over the years. As I look back at all the mistakes I've made, I'm amazed that I didn't stop cooking altogether. But the desire to get people together, to share a meal, overcame any reluctance to cook or any embarrassment about a less than perfect dish.

When I got into the kitchen with these talented chefs, I learned technique, but I learned something about myself too. When seafood expert Eric Ripert, the chef of one of America's best restaurants, Le Bernardin, taught me the humane way to kill a lobster—swiftly, with a knife through its spinal cord—I took three tries to pierce the shell. His assessment of my mistake was simple. I wasn't present. "Your mind was everywhere but the tip of that knife," he said. And in that moment I felt completely exposed. I'd thought I had put all my energy into the task at hand, but Eric saw right through me. He recognized my uncertainty (can I really do this?); he sensed my mind wandering as I thought about the finished dish, work that wasn't getting done and fifty other things. He made it clear that one of the most critical skills in cooking is learning to focus.

When I was in the kitchen with Kristen Kish, the winner of *Top Chef* season 10, impatience was my downfall. We were browning chicken for the recipe on page 102. I kept asking, "Is it ready yet?" "No," came the answer repeatedly. I wanted to get on with it—after all, the chicken was just going to simmer. But Kristen insisted that shortcuts would negatively affect the final taste.

David Chang, the genius behind the Momofuku empire, taught me another important life lesson when we were making kimchi. He explained how to cut cucumbers for a more advanced version of the recipe in the book. I only half paid attention, because I was sure I knew what he wanted. Without watching what he did, I made four parallel cuts. David looked over and his eyes almost popped out of his head. He had asked me to cut a cross into the vegetable so it could be stuffed with a chunky marinade. My cucumbers were impossible to stuff. I didn't listen to the steps David outlined or observe what he did, so I made a dumb mistake. In life, as in the kitchen, you always need to listen and not make assumptions.

The chef lessons turned into life lessons. Now, when I cook, I hear the chefs in my head saying, "Slow down, stay focused." But I also hear them talking to me at other times—when I'm with my family, say, or in a meeting. I apply what I learned from them in the kitchen to every aspect of my life: be present, pay attention, listen, have patience.

I embarked on this journey to master my mistakes in the kitchen and share what I learned with you, dear reader, so you could master your own kitchen mistakes. Along the way, I discovered a bigger lesson—something more important than the perfect fried chicken or no-fail soufflé. And that is to be honest about what holds you back—in the kitchen and in life—and face it head-on.

WHAT I'VE LEARNED: A CHEAT SHEET

By cooking with star chefs and writing down and analyzing my mistakes in the kitchen, I learned a lot about myself and about making great food. If you follow these tips, you will be well on your way to be becoming a great cook, too.

READ EACH RECIPE CAREFULLY THROUGH TO THE END BEFORE YOU START. I've heard this piece of advice ever since I started cooking. But as I (somewhat) more scientifically examined my mistakes, I realized I wasn't paying attention as diligently as I had thought. Double-check:

- Do you have all the ingredients you need?
- Do you have all the equipment you need?
- Do you have all the time you need, including time to let the dish rest?

DON'T BE LAZY. I used to skip steps that seemed to take too much effort or didn't seem worthwhile. I was wrong. I just didn't understand the ramifications. So I exhort you:

- When making cookies and cakes, bring all of your ingredients to room temperature. As Hedy Goldsmith of Michael's Genuine Food & Drink in Miami said, "Cold ingredients are a fail waiting to happen."
- When baking, turn the pan or pans for more even cooking; all ovens have hot spots.
- When cooking meat, whether it's beef, duck, lamb or chicken, bring it to room temperature so it will cook evenly.
- When roasting vegetables, turn them often so they don't burn and so they cook evenly.

DON'T BE IMPATIENT. I realized that I was often in a rush when I was cooking. Even when I wasn't in a rush, I was moving quickly so I could get on to other things. This leads to less-than-excellent results. If you take shortcuts, they will often compromise your outcome. For example:

- When creaming butter and sugar, beat them long enough so they're fluffy and light in texture and color.
- When browning meat, give it time to really caramelize before you move to your next step. Cooking is about developing and layering flavor, and browning develops those flavors. And don't crowd the pan—foods should not be touching each other, or they will steam, not brown; if necessary, use two pans or brown in batches.
- When cooking meat, allow for adequate resting time.
- When baking, let breads and other baked goods cool properly.

ACT WITH CONVICTION. When I was cooking with the chefs, I was impressed by their lack of tolerance for a casual approach to cooking. Eric Ripert corrected me when I was gently whisking a sauce for lobster (see page 179). I wasn't focused, and he urged me to be more aggressive. Good chefs focus mightily when they're in the kitchen. You need to, too.

TAKE THE EXTRA TIME TO MAKE A DISH TASTE GREAT.
- To get crispy skin on poultry, allow birds to rest, uncovered, in the refrigerator overnight if possible before cooking, to reduce the moisture in their skin. The drier you can get it, the better the final result. Daniel Humm recommends this for duck (see page 132), Thomas Keller for chicken (see page 122) and Jonathan Waxman for turkey (see page 130).
- To get the seasoning right in a ground meat mixture, cook off a little tester in a skillet to taste so you can adjust the seasoning if necessary before continuing with the recipe. Ming Tsai recommends this for Pot Stickers (page 23), Daniel Holzman for Pork Meatball Sliders (page 27) and Edward Lee for Korean Meat Loaf (page 148).

MAKE SURE YOU USE THE RIGHT EQUIPMENT.
- For baking sheets, make sure they're sturdy, or they will buckle, twist or heat up unevenly. Commercial-grade sheets are great for just about everything, including roasting vegetables (see page 62) and baking granola (see page 222). Buy pro-style baking sheets at restaurant supply stores. You'll have them for life.

- For consistent portions, use ice cream scoops. Daniel Holzman recommends this for meatballs (see page 27) and Cheryl Day does for cookies (see page 258). This guarantees that everything will be the same size and will cook or bake evenly.

GET TO KNOW YOUR OVEN. In many ovens, the gauge on the outside does not accurately reflect the temperature on the inside. The first step is to get a good oven thermometer. Thomas Keller told me, "You don't necessarily need to fix your oven if it's off; just make sure it's at the temperature you need by checking the thermometer, even if it means adjusting your dial." And, of course, if you have the time and energy, get your oven recalibrated. The wrong oven temperature can ruin an otherwise well-executed dish.

DON'T FOLLOW YOUR INSTINCTS UNTIL YOUR INSTINCTS ARE DEVELOPED. Some of my most cringe-inducing moments in cooking have been when I realized my "smart" adjustment was actually a big mistake, as in when I added the extra juices to the beef as it was being seared (see page 158). I still wince when I think about it.

THINK ABOUT SAFETY. Even the most macho chefs were very clear about safety. A few rules to always follow:

- Place your knife, blade facing away from you, at the top of your cutting board when it's not in use.
- Lift the lid on a pot of boiling liquid facing away from you to avoid a steam burn.
- Flip foods, like fish, steaks or fillets, away from you so you don't get splattered when they land.
- Tie a towel around the handle of a hot pan so that you don't burn yourself when you pick it up.

**cheese soufflé,
page 10**

starters + soups

cheese soufflé · 10

salsamole · 13

spicy spiced nuts · 14

bruschetta española · 17

tuna + white bean "tonnato" dip · 20

pot stickers · 23

pork meatball sliders · 27

chicken soup four ways · 29

spring chicken soup with asparagus, peas, orzo + dill · 29

summer chicken soup with zucchini, spinach, rice + basil · 30

fall chicken soup with lemon, egg + fontina · 30

winter asian chicken soup · 31

udon noodle soup · 32

spicy watermelon gazpacho · 35

lentil + swiss chard soup with lemon · 36

creamy roasted carrot soup with pine nut + caper topping · 39

Cheese Soufflé

66 For a Valentine's Day many years ago, I wanted to make a special dinner for a new boyfriend. A shared soufflé served with a green salad seemed the perfect choice. I focused most of my attention on the décor, not the food. Everything matched—I even used ticket stubs from the movie my boyfriend and I had seen on our first date to make placemats. I didn't really think too much about the fact that I'd never made a soufflé before. I only discovered the finickiness of the dish while whipping the egg whites. Hard as I tried, they wouldn't rise to a stiff peak. When I brought the finished dish to the table, it looked a lot more like a frittata than a soufflé. Instead of laughing at the deflated mess, my boyfriend said he loved it. That's the kind of eater who's a keeper in my book—and, in fact, that accepting boyfriend is now my husband.

When I described my problems to the world's greatest cooking teacher, Jacques Pépin, he let me in on his no-fail soufflé secret: Use cream cheese to stabilize the mixture. I've incorporated that *truc* in the recipe below.

ACTIVE TIME: 20 MINUTES   TOTAL TIME: 45 MINUTES
SERVES 2

1 tablespoon unsalted butter, plus more for the ramekins
1 tablespoon finely grated Parmigiano-Reggiano cheese
1 tablespoon all-purpose flour
¼ cup whole milk
2 tablespoons cream cheese, at room temperature
1 large egg yolk
¾ teaspoon kosher salt
¼ cup lightly packed shredded aged Gouda cheese
2 large egg whites

1 Position a rack in the lower third of the oven and preheat the oven to 400°F.

2 Generously butter two 6-ounce ramekins. Add half of the Parmigiano-Reggiano to each and tilt the ramekins to coat the bottoms and sides. Set them on a rimmed baking sheet.

3 Melt the tablespoon of butter in a medium heavy saucepan over medium heat. Add the flour and cook, whisking, until the mixture begins to foam and turn very light brown, about 2 minutes. Slowly add the milk, whisking constantly until smooth, then whisk in the cream cheese until it is incorporated and the mixture is thickened. Scrape the mixture into a large bowl. Whisk it for a minute to cool it down, then whisk in the egg yolk, salt and Gouda until well incorporated.

4 Put the egg whites in the bowl of a stand mixer (or use a large bowl and a handheld mixer) and beat them just until they're stiff.

5 Using a rubber spatula, fold one-third of the whipped egg whites into the soufflé base until incorporated, then fold in the remaining egg whites until no streaks remain, being careful not to lose any of the air you just painstakingly beat into them. Divide the mixture between the prepared ramekins.

6 Transfer the baking sheet to the oven and immediately turn the temperature down to 375°F. Bake until the soufflés are puffed and golden brown on top, 20 to 25 minutes. Remove the soufflés from the oven and serve immediately.

NOTE Don't open the oven door until you're ready to remove the soufflés—check them through the window. Opening the door creates temperature fluctuations, which can cause the soufflés to fall.

chef tips from jacques pépin

ON PREPPING THE SOUFFLÉ DISHES Make sure the soufflé dishes are well buttered so the soufflés won't stick to them.

ON TIMING THE SOUFFLÉ PREP Make the soufflé base before you start beating the egg whites. Once the egg whites are whipped, you want to incorporate them into the base mixture immediately so as not to lose any of the air.

ON BAKING Put the ramekins on a baking sheet so that the heat is evenly distributed and it's easier to get the soufflés out of the oven.

ON TIMING People should wait for a soufflé; a soufflé waits for no one!

SOUFFLÉ SERVING SIZE The smaller the mold, the less likely the soufflé will crack. Individual-sized ramekins, as in the recipe here, are the safest. If you want to make a soufflé in one big dish, you can make a nice soufflé for six, but don't attempt one for twenty.

Salsamole

❝ There may be some reasonable debate about whether or not the avocado-onion-lime dip that I made for a recent cocktail party was technically a guacamole. But there was no debate that it was seriously lacking. I asked a guest who had arrived early for her opinion. "Needs salt." OK, I said, and added more. I asked another guest what she thought. "Needs acid," she said. I added more lime. The next guest, a precocious sixteen-year-old, offered me his own recipe, which included tomatoes, hot peppers and cilantro and sounded a lot like the salsa that was also on the buffet (minus the avocado). So I boldly folded the salsa into the "guacamole." When I asked yet another guest what he thought of the salsamole, he just smiled, ignorant of the controversy, and said, "Tastes great!" I asked Susan Feniger, of Border Grill in LA, for her tips. Number one on her list: make the salsamole with grilled Hass avocados (see Chef Tips, below right).

TOTAL TIME: 15 MINUTES   SERVES 8

....

2 ripe tomatoes, diced
1 cup finely diced seeded cucumber (about ½ large English cucumber)
¼ cup finely diced white onion
½ jalapeño, seeded and finely diced
¼ cup cilantro leaves, finely chopped
½ teaspoon fine salt, or more to taste
3 tablespoons freshly squeezed lime juice, or more to taste
2 ripe Hass avocados, halved, pitted, peeled and roughly diced
Tortilla chips, for serving

Put the tomatoes, cucumber, onion, jalapeño, cilantro, salt and lime juice in a medium bowl and toss well. Add the avocado and toss well to combine. Season to taste with more salt and/or lime juice if necessary. Serve immediately, with tortilla chips.

WHY DIDN'T I THINK OF THAT?
MORE RECIPE IDEAS FROM SUSAN FENIGER

- Add chopped roasted chiles to the guacamole.
- For a smoky flavor, make the guacamole with grilled avocados.
- Halve an avocado and drizzle with extra-virgin olive oil and salt for a great breakfast or snack.
- Puree avocados with roasted tomatillos and use as a sauce instead of a dip.

chef tips from **susan feniger**

ON THE BEST AVOCADOS FOR GUACAMOLE California Hass avocados are the best for guacamole because their fat content is high, giving them great richness.

ON CHECKING FOR RIPENESS To tell if an avocado is ripe and perfect for guacamole, hold it in the palm of your hand and gently squeeze it. Don't squeeze with your fingertips, because that can bruise the fruit. You're looking for it to barely give.

Spicy Spiced Nuts

66 There are few recipes as beloved by *Food & Wine* editors as the spiced nuts from Wente Vineyards. We published the recipe more than ten years ago, and it remains a staff favorite for holiday gifts and parties. Their universal popularity, the short ingredient list and simple instructions gave me the confidence that I could make the nuts without any mistakes. They were good—really good—but I wanted a stronger whiff of heat and some smoke. I upped the cayenne and added pimentón (smoked Spanish paprika). So first I mastered the nuts, and then I made them my own.

ACTIVE TIME. 15 MINUTES   TOTAL TIME: 35 MINUTES, PLUS COOLING
MAKES 6 CUPS

....

¼ cup pure maple syrup
2 tablespoons extra-virgin olive oil
2 tablespoons minced rosemary
½ teaspoon cayenne pepper
¾ teaspoon dulce pimentón de la Vera (smoked Spanish paprika)
1 teaspoon kosher salt
6 cups mixed raw nuts, such as pecans, almonds, cashews and
    walnuts

1 Preheat the oven to 350°F. Line a baking sheet with parchment paper.
2 Stir together the maple syrup, olive oil, rosemary, cayenne, pimentón and salt in a large bowl. Stir in the nuts, making sure each one is well coated.
3 Spread the nuts on the prepared baking sheet and bake, stirring after 10 minutes, until they smell roasted and look browned, about 20 minutes. Transfer the baking sheet to a cooling rack and allow the nuts to cool completely (they will crisp as they cool).

NOTE If you prefer even spicier nuts, you can increase the cayenne to ¾ teaspoon to 1 teaspoon.
MAKE AHEAD Once cooled completely, the nuts can be stored in an airtight container or resealable plastic bag for up to 2 weeks.

Bruschetta Española

66 Soon after volunteering to turn my friend Chris's home-grown tomatoes into bruschetta for a big family-style lunch, I regretted it. Before I could head out to the grill, it started to rain. Hard. But I didn't want to disappoint, so I sliced a baguette, ran to the grill, shoved the bread on the grate and then took it off as soon as possible. Back in the kitchen, I prepped the tomato mixture, put it onto the toasts and set the bruschetta on the sideboard, hoping no one would notice that the bread lacked that signature toastiness and had gone cold.

After that experience, I consulted Spain's unofficial ambassador of food, José Andrés, whom I've watched transform tomatoes at many cooking demonstrations. He revolutionized this simple dish for me forever. First he suggested using sliced sourdough bread, not a baguette, because it toasts more evenly. And then he suggested using a toaster oven instead of the grill. A sacrilege, or so I thought, until he demonstrated how evenly bread browns in the toaster oven and how unevenly it is toasts on a grill. Then came the signature José move: he removed the flavorful clusters of seeds that he calls the "caviar" from some of the tomatoes and placed them just so on top of the chopped tomatoes on half of the toasts. This last bit is optional, but I'm now convinced that toasting bread for bruschetta is the way to go—not just when it's raining.

TOTAL TIME: 15 MINUTES   SERVES 4

....

¼ cup olive oil

1 garlic clove, crushed

4 slices sourdough bread (¼ to ½ inch thick)

½ pound ripe tomatoes, chopped, plus optional Campari or
    large cherry tomatoes for topping (see Note)

1 teaspoon thyme leaves, finely chopped

1 teaspoon sherry vinegar

Kosher salt

1 Put the olive oil and crushed garlic clove in a medium bowl and let sit for at least 10 minutes.

2 Toast the bread in a toaster oven until golden brown. Brush with some of the garlic-infused oil.

3 Remove and discard the garlic clove from the remaining oil and add the tomatoes, thyme and vinegar to the bowl. Toss to combine and season to taste with salt.

4 Pile the tomato mixture on the toasts and serve immediately.

NOTE To prepare this dish as José does, cut away the skin and flesh of Campari or large cherry tomatoes, leaving behind the seedy centers. Use the centers (the "caviar") as a garnish and then finely chop the firmer tomato flesh to add to the tomato mixture.

chef tips from **josé andrés**

ON TOASTING BREAD The best way to toast bread at home is in a toaster oven. Toast offers a life lesson: be hard on the outside, soft on the inside.

ON THE BEST TOMATOES FOR BRUSCHETTA Use the ripest tomatoes possible—even the overripe ones that the farmers are throwing out at the end of the day at the market, the ones that are the consistency of a canned tomato in a fresh tomato. And the tomatoes should be extremely heavy for their size, an indication of all of the juice inside.

ON GARLIC For just a touch of garlic, instead of rubbing the bread with a garlic clove, smash the clove and drop it in olive oil to subtly flavor the oil.

ON FIXING A TOMATO TOPPING WITH TOO MUCH VINEGAR If you add too much vinegar by mistake, just change the name to vinegar-infused tomatoes!

Tuna + White Bean "Tonnato" Dip

> **❝** I have a recurring dream in which friends come over unexpectedly and I have to create an impromptu meal. In the dream, I just grab pasta and tomato sauce and put them together for a fast meal. But recently, my dreams took a turn for the better when I made up a dish in my sleep that I still liked when I woke up. It was a super-versatile tuna dip made with canned white beans, lemon, olive oil, salt and mayo. Those are the flavors in the classic sauce for *vitello tonnato*—cold veal with a creamy tuna puree. This dip can also be used as a spread or sauce, or even in a tuna melt.

TOTAL TIME: 15 MINUTES   MAKES ABOUT 2 CUPS

One 15-ounce can white beans, drained and rinsed
One 7-ounce can water-packed tuna, drained
3 tablespoons extra-virgin olive oil, plus more for drizzling
3 tablespoons mayonnaise
1 teaspoon finely grated lemon zest
3 tablespoons freshly squeezed lemon juice
½ teaspoon kosher salt
¼ teaspoon cayenne pepper, plus more for sprinkling
¼ teaspoon crushed red pepper

Put all of the ingredients in the bowl of a food processor and puree until smooth. Transfer to a serving bowl, drizzle with olive oil and sprinkle with cayenne.

SERVE WITH Raw vegetables, flatbread or chips.
MAKE AHEAD The dip can be refrigerated for up to 3 days.

MORE USES FOR TONNATO DIP

- Spread on toast and top with sliced radishes and chopped celery leaves.
- Make a modern tuna melt by spreading the dip on bread, draping it with cheese and broiling.
- Use in a tomato sandwich.

Pot Stickers

66 Before starting treatment for breast cancer about seven years ago, I researched the effects of chemotherapy, among other things, and I tried to make peace with what I learned—including the idea that I would lose my hair and my appetite. As it turned out, though, I was a very hungry cancer patient. Pot stickers were a particular craving. So I started making them myself, adapting Ming Tsai's recipe that appeared in *Food & Wine*. While mine were tasty, they never achieved that satisfying yum of a dim-sum-parlor dumpling. The bottoms browned but didn't stay crisp, and the filling wasn't juicy. Then I learned from Ming to use a lot of vegetables in the filling to make it juicier and to brown the pot stickers in the pan before steaming them and then crisp them a second time.

TOTAL TIME: 1 HOUR   MAKES 40 POT STICKERS

FOR THE DIPPING SAUCE

1 tablespoon Sriracha

¼ cup + 2 tablespoons soy sauce

¼ cup rice vinegar

2 tablespoons water

1 teaspoon Asian sesame oil

1 tablespoon thinly sliced scallions

FOR THE POT STICKERS

6 ounces ground pork

6 ounces medium shrimp, shelled, deveined and finely chopped

4 ounces soft tofu

¾ cup finely chopped scallions

1½ tablespoons minced peeled ginger

2 garlic cloves, minced

2 tablespoons soy sauce

1 tablespoon Asian sesame oil

¾ teaspoon kosher salt

½ teaspoon freshly ground black pepper

1 package (at least 40) fresh round dumpling wrappers (3½ inches in diameter)

Vegetable oil, for frying

1 For the dipping sauce, stir all of the ingredients together in a bowl; set aside.

2 Put the pork and shrimp in a large bowl. Wrap the tofu in cheesecloth or a clean kitchen towel. Wring out the moisture (so your pot stickers don't get soggy), then crumble the tofu into the bowl. Mix in the scallions, ginger, garlic, soy sauce, sesame oil, salt and pepper.

3 Lay a few dumpling wrappers on a dry work surface (keep the rest covered with a damp paper towel) and top each one with a scant tablespoon of filling, right in the center of the wrapper. Set out a little bowl of water and, using your fingertip, brush the edges of the wrappers with water. Fold each one into a half-moon and seal the edges tightly together, making sure to press out any air. Starting at the center of each pot sticker, pleat the sealed edges, making up to 8 pleats. Then pick up each pot sticker by the pleats and tap it on your work surface to give it a flat bottom. Transfer the pot stickers to a baking sheet lined with plastic wrap and cover them with a damp paper towel. Continue forming pot stickers until you've used up all of the filling.

4 Heat 1½ tablespoons of vegetable oil in a large heavy nonstick skillet over medium-high heat until shimmering. Place 12 of the pot stickers, flattened bottom down, in the skillet and cook until the bottoms are browned, about 2 minutes.

5 Hold a lid at an angle over the skillet, so you don't get splattered, and pour ½ cup of water into the pan. Immediately cover the skillet and cook until steam stops rising. Remove the lid and cook just until the bottoms of the pot stickers are crisp again, another 2 minutes.

6 Using a thin spatula, transfer the pot stickers to a serving plate. Serve immediately, with the dipping sauce. Wipe out the skillet and repeat the cooking process, serving each batch as you go so that the pot stickers can be eaten while they are hot.

MAKE AHEAD Uncooked pot stickers can be frozen for up to 1 month. Freeze in a single layer on a baking sheet lined with plastic wrap until frozen hard, then transfer to a resealable plastic bag. Do not thaw before cooking.

chef tips from **ming tsai**

ON HOW TO GET THE JUICIEST DUMPLINGS Use ground pork and lots of juicy vegetables like scallions, carrots and cabbage, which will release moisture as they cook.

ON THE BEST DUMPLING WRAPPERS Buy fresh, not frozen, dumpling wrappers at an Asian market. The thinnest ones make the best dumplings.

ON PLEATING THE DUMPLINGS Make sure each dumpling has at least 5 pleats to secure it. I do 8 pleats for feng shui reasons—everyone needs good chi!

ON WHICH PAN TO USE Use a cast-iron or other heavy-bottomed skillet for the best results.

ON THE OPTIMAL HEAT Cook over medium-high heat. If the pan is too hot, the dumplings will get crisp and dark too quickly.

ON STEAMING DUMPLINGS Have water or low-sodium chicken broth (for extra richness) and a lid at the ready. As soon as you achieve the perfect color and crispiness, add the liquid, with the lid half covering the pan angled away from you so you don't get splattered.

ON COOKING FROZEN DUMPLINGS Cook frozen dumplings in the same way but over slightly lower heat to allow them to thaw as they cook. If you defrost them, they will get mushy and the skins will tear . . . *no bueno!*

Pork Meatball Sliders

❝ I was superexcited, and a little nervous. Danny Meyer, the impresario behind many of New York's best restaurants and the Shake Shack burger empire, was coming to my house upstate with his family before a theater outing. Danny's wife, Audrey, was starring in *Damn Yankees*, which was playing nearby. I fretted for weeks about what to serve. Sliders were the answer: not too much food, not too little. I was ready with two different versions when they arrived. It wasn't until Danny took his first bite that it dawned on me that I was serving mini burgers to the king of burgers!

One slider was a sausage and beef blend; it was disappointing because the sausage was lackluster. However, the punchy giardiniera condiment on top was terrific. The second slider was a riff on a spectacular Andrew Carmellini recipe in *Food & Wine* that included pork, bacon and prosciutto, sun-dried tomatoes and milk-soaked bread. Because of all the tasty ingredients, I didn't bother to add any condiments. The sliders were great, but Danny missed the crunch of the pickle-y sauce. With his guidance, I combined the best of both and arrived at my new signature slider.

For a master class in mini-burger making, I reached out to Daniel Holzman of The Meatball Shop in New York City. He gave me excellent advice: always cook off a tester patty first. That way, you can adjust the seasoning before you cook all the sliders.

ACTIVE TIME: 30 MINUTES   TOTAL TIME: 1 HOUR   MAKES 15 SLIDERS

FOR THE MEATBALLS

Three ½-inch-thick slices day-old white sandwich bread, crusts removed, bread chopped into small pieces (1½ cups)

⅓ cup whole milk

1 large egg, lightly beaten

2 tablespoons finely chopped flat-leaf parsley

2 tablespoons finely chopped basil

2 tablespoons finely grated Pecorino cheese

½ teaspoon kosher salt, or more to taste

½ teaspoon freshly ground black pepper, or more to taste

½ pound ground pork

½ pound sweet Italian sausages, casings removed, sausage crumbled

chef tips from
daniel holzman

ON MAKING LIGHT AND TENDER MEATBALLS Add bread, cooked rice or another filler. The higher the percentage of lean meat to filler, the denser the meatball.

ON SHAPING PERFECT BALLS Portion the meatballs with an ice cream scoop, then roll them between your palms to make perfectly round balls— don't be afraid to apply a little force.

AVOID OVERCOOKING Use an instant-read thermometer, and take the meatballs out when they reach 150°F.

FOR THE GIARDINIERA SPECIAL SAUCE
½ cup mayonnaise
½ cup finely chopped giardiniera (pickled vegetables, available jarred or at the olive bar at supermarkets and Italian markets)
1½ tablespoons giardiniera pickling liquid
1½ tablespoons ketchup

TO SERVE
15 soft slider buns
1½ cups roughly chopped arugula

1 Preheat the oven to 425°F. Line a large rimmed baking sheet with parchment paper.

2 Put the bread in a large bowl, add the milk, and let the bread sit until it's softened, about 2 minutes. Scrunch the bread with your hands so that it almost forms a paste. Add the egg, parsley, basil, Pecorino, salt and pepper and mix until uniformly combined. Add the ground pork and sausage and knead gently to combine.

3 Fry a little tester patty in a skillet and adjust the seasonings as necessary.

4 Use a small (2-tablespoon-size) ice cream scoop to form the pork mixture into 30 small meatballs. Gently roll each meatball in your hands until smooth. Line them up on the prepared baking sheet, leaving a little space between them.

5 Bake until the meatballs are just firm and an instant-read thermometer inserted in the middle of the meatball in the center of the baking sheet registers 150°F, about 15 minutes.

6 Meanwhile, put all the ingredients for the sauce in a small bowl and stir together.

7 Top the bottom of each slider bun with 2 meatballs and some arugula. Add on plenty of giardiniera sauce and the tops of the buns and serve.

MAKE AHEAD The giardiniera sauce can be refrigerated for up to 3 days.

Chicken Soup Four Ways

"Everyone, including neophyte cooks, has at least one recipe that works every time. For me, that recipe is chicken noodle soup. When my kids were little, we made chicken soup almost every weekend. We started with College Inn chicken broth, the kind I grew up with, and improvised, depending on what was in the fridge. The kids chose which pasta to add; I insisted on something green like snap peas, green beans, spinach or broccoli (my son, William, always left these at the bottom of his bowl). Occasionally we'd make an Asian version, tossing in tofu and edamame. One of the few recipes in my husband Barclay's repertoire is also chicken soup. He adds cheese, egg and lemon for a terrific fall version. I've stolen his recipe here. But for even more fantastic and original chicken soup ideas, I went to the incomparable Grant Achatz of Alinea in Chicago.

Spring Chicken Soup with Asparagus, Peas, Orzo + Dill

TOTAL TIME: 20 MINUTES   SERVES 4

4 cups chicken stock or low-sodium chicken broth
½ cup orzo
8 spears asparagus, tough ends snapped off, spears roughly chopped
½ cup fresh or frozen peas
Fine salt and freshly ground black pepper
¼ cup finely chopped dill

1 Pour the chicken stock into a medium pot and bring to a boil. Add the orzo and cook for 2 minutes less than the package instructs.
2 Add the asparagus and peas and simmer until they're bright green, about 2 minutes. Season with salt and pepper and stir in the dill. Ladle the soup into bowls and serve.

Summer Chicken Soup with Zucchini, Spinach, Rice + Basil

TOTAL TIME: 20 MINUTES SERVES 4

....

4 cups chicken stock or low-sodium chicken broth
½ cup long-grain white rice, rinsed well
1 small zucchini, cut into ¼-inch dice
3 loosely packed cups baby spinach leaves
Fine salt and freshly ground black pepper
12 large basil leaves, finely sliced

1 Pour the chicken stock into a medium pot and bring to a boil. Add the rice and cook for 3 minutes less than the package instructs.
2 Add the zucchini and cook until tender, about 2 minutes. Stir in the spinach and cook until wilted, about 1 minute. Make sure the rice is tender, then season the soup with salt and pepper. Ladle the soup into bowls, garnish with the basil and serve.

Fall Chicken Soup with Lemon, Egg + Fontina

TOTAL TIME: 15 MINUTES SERVES 4

....

4 cups chicken stock or low-sodium chicken broth
2 tablespoons freshly squeezed lemon juice
Fine salt and freshly ground black pepper
2 large eggs, beaten
½ cup shredded Fontina cheese
¼ cup freshly grated Parmesan cheese

1 Pour the chicken stock into a medium pot and bring to a boil. Lower the heat to a simmer, stir in the lemon juice and season with salt and pepper.
2 While stirring, slowly pour the eggs into the soup—they will spread out and feather. Ladle the soup into bowls, top each with the cheese and serve immediately.

Winter Asian Chicken Soup

TOTAL TIME: 15 MINUTES   SERVES 4

4 cups chicken stock or low-sodium chicken broth
1 cup finely diced carrots
1 tablespoon minced peeled ginger
Half a 14-ounce package firm tofu, drained and cubed
1 cup frozen shelled edamame
1½ tablespoons soy sauce
1½ tablespoons mirin
Asian chile-garlic sauce, for serving

1 Pour the chicken stock into a medium pot and bring to a boil. Lower the heat to medium, add the carrots and ginger and cook, stirring occasionally, until tender, about 5 minutes.

2 Stir in the tofu, edamame, soy sauce and mirin and cook for just another couple of minutes to warm everything through. Ladle the soup into bowls and serve, passing chile-garlic sauce at the table.

WHY DIDN'T I THINK OF THAT?
MORE RECIPE IDEAS FROM GRANT ACHATZ

CLEAR CHICKEN SOUP

- Chicken and Sweet Corn Broth with cumin and crème fraîche dumplings: Using corn cobs as you would soup bones, fortify the basic chicken broth into a sweeter, more aromatic liquid and then add richness with the cumin-infused dumplings.

ROBUST CHICKEN SOUP

- Chicken and Eggplant Velouté with coriander, white pepper and burnt sugar: This is a Thai riff on a catfish dish we did at Next using a white pepper, coriander and caramel sauce, which sounds strange but really works.

CHILLED CHICKEN SOUP

- Chilled Chicken and Almond Milk with roasted peppers and olives: A combination of almond milk and chicken stock goes to the Mediterranean with olives, oregano, saffron and roasted peppers. A white chicken gazpacho in a way.

Udon Noodle Soup

" For my daughter's eleventh-birthday sleepover party, Sylvie really wanted to order udon noodle soup from her favorite Japanese restaurant. But I wouldn't hear of it. I didn't want the takeout version, with its MSG-laden broth, bad chicken and weird canned mushrooms. I couldn't imagine that making udon noodle soup would be so different from chicken noodle soup, which I had mastered long ago (see Chicken Soup Four Ways, page 29). Shopping like a pro, I went out of my way to go to the best Japanese grocery store to buy authentic noodles and pickles, and I bought organic chicken and three kinds of vegetables. But after all that, the broth was mysteriously flavorless, the vegetables were undercooked and the udon was overcooked.

According to Paul Qui, of Qui in Austin, Texas, I could have achieved the richer flavor I wanted by including a fermented ingredient, like sauerkraut, at the end. Odd as that sounded, I added a little of the funky cabbage to my next batch of soup and was dazzled by the improvement.

ACTIVE TIME: 15 MINUTES   TOTAL TIME: 35 MINUTES   SERVES 4

6 cups chicken stock or low-sodium chicken broth
8 dried shiitake mushrooms
One 6-inch piece dried kombu (see Notes), rinsed
¼ cup soy sauce
¼ cup mirin
3 tablespoons sake (optional)
Kosher salt
Four 8-ounce packets fresh-frozen udon noodles (see Notes)
1 bunch enoki mushrooms, root ends trimmed off,
    cut crosswise in half
½ cup drained sauerkraut
4 small scallions, thinly sliced
1 small rotisserie chicken, meat pulled from the bones and
    coarsely shredded (optional)

1 Pour the chicken stock into a large saucepan and bring to a boil over high heat. Lower the heat to a simmer, add the shiitake mushrooms and kombu and cook until the broth is infused with the flavor of the mushrooms and kombu and the mushrooms are totally softened, about 10 minutes.

2 Use a slotted spoon to remove and discard the kombu. Using the spoon, transfer the mushrooms to a cutting board and let them cool. Stir the soy sauce, mirin and sake, if using, into the broth, season with salt and keep warm over low heat.

3 Bring a large saucepan of water to a boil.

4 Meanwhile, once the shiitakes are cool enough to handle, trim off and discard the stems. Thinly slice the caps and set aside.

5 Cook the udon noodles in the boiling water according to the package directions. Drain the noodles and divide them evenly among four bowls.

6 Top the noodles with the reserved shiitakes, the enoki mushrooms, sauerkraut, scallions and chicken, if using. Ladle the broth into the bowls and serve immediately.

SERVE WITH *Togarashi*, a Japanese seasoning blend that includes ground chiles, sesame seeds and dried orange peel.

NOTES Kombu, a dried seaweed, can be found in the ethnic aisle of most grocery stores, at your local Asian market or online at edenfoods.com. Fresh-frozen udon noodles are available at Asian markets.

MAKE AHEAD The broth can be refrigerated for up to 3 days; reheat before serving.

chef tips from **paul qui**

ON THE BEST NOODLES Use fresh-frozen udon noodles instead of dried. They're the same kind you find in Japanese restaurants. The key is not to cook them too much, just 20 or 30 seconds—the noodles are already cooked, you're just warming them through.

ON ADDING FLAVOR TO STORE-BOUGHT CHICKEN BROTH Incorporate a fermented food, like sauerkraut, pickles, kimchi or miso.

Spicy Watermelon Gazpacho

" When I realized that gazpacho is like a savory version of the sweet blender drinks my cooking-challenged mother made when I was growing up (see page 227), I was emboldened. I figured I could whip up a big batch for a crowd. Using a recipe from the divine brother duo of Matt Lee and Ted Lee as the foundation, I plunged ahead with a watermelon and tomato soup, changing out some of the ingredients. It came together satisfyingly easily. But when I tasted it, it was way too sweet. I hadn't taken into account the amount of natural sugar in the watermelon I was using. This failure served as an indelible reminder that ingredients are not always the same, so you need to taste as you go. To learn more about making gazpacho, I got advice from Alex Raij of La Vara in Brooklyn, New York, whose Spanish food is simple and delicious.

TOTAL TIME: 30 MINUTES + AT LEAST 2 HOURS CHILLING
SERVES 4 TO 6

FOR THE GAZPACHO
2 pounds ripe plum tomatoes (6 large tomatoes), roughly chopped
1½ pounds peeled seedless watermelon, cut into 1-inch chunks (about 4 cups)
2 tablespoons Sriracha, plus more to taste
2 small garlic cloves, minced
¼ cup freshly squeezed lime juice, plus more to taste
2 teaspoons salt, plus more to taste
¾ cup buttermilk, plus (optional) more for drizzling

GARNISHES
Diced avocado, cilantro leaves, thinly sliced scallions, crabmeat

1 For the gazpacho, toss all of the ingredients together in a large bowl. Transfer half of the mixture to a blender and puree until smooth.
2 Press the gazpacho with a ladle or wooden spoon through a medium strainer into a pitcher or serving bowl; discard the contents of the strainer. (If you prefer a chunkier texture, you can skip the straining. Ditto if you have a superpowerful blender like a Vitamix.) Repeat with the remaining tomato mixture. Refrigerate the gazpacho for at least 2 hours before serving.
3 Stir the gazpacho and season with additional Sriracha, lime juice and salt as necessary. Serve ice-cold, topped with garnishes.

chef tips from
alex raij

ON GETTING THE BEST, CREAMIEST CONSISTENCY Use a blender, not a food processor—ideally, a Vitamix.

ON EXTRACTING THE MOST TOMATO FLAVOR Use the whole tomato—you can always strain out what you don't want, but the seeds and skin have a lot of acidity, complexity of flavor and textural assets to contribute.

GAZPACHO VARIATIONS
- Cherry and tomato gazpacho
- Strawberry and tomato gazpacho
- Cantaloupe gazpacho—because cantaloupe is the melon that most closely resembles the texture of a cucumber, an ingredient in classic gazpachos, and because Spain has amazing melons!
- For an even smoother and richer gazpacho, add ½ cup olive oil in a thin stream, as per a vinaigrette, while the blender is running.

Lentil + Swiss Chard Soup with Lemon

" For a small dinner party one snowy winter evening, I embarked on making a lentil soup with Swiss chard, modeled on a *Food & Wine* recipe from Bay Area chef Tasha Prysi. I inadvertently cut back the liquid, though, and ended up making something very different. I simmered the lentils for the specified 30 minutes, yet when I checked on them, they were still tough. I continued to simmer them over low heat, but by the time they were cooked through, they'd gorged on the water and chicken broth—my soup had disappeared and what remained was a (perfectly cooked) lentil side dish. I quizzed Tina Ujlaki, *F&W*'s executive food editor, and she gave me embarrassingly simple advice: to make that side dish into soup, just add water. (I don't know why I didn't think of it at the time—I blame it on the pressure of a dinner party.) This recipe makes a lovely soup, but, if you're in the mood for a lentil side dish, just cut the liquid back to 3 cups total.

ACTIVE TIME: 30 MINUTES   TOTAL TIME: 1¼ HOURS   SERVES 4

3 tablespoons olive oil

½ large yellow onion, finely chopped

1 garlic clove, minced

Pinch of crushed red pepper

¼ cup coarsely chopped cilantro

Kosher salt

1 cup de Puy or beluga lentils (firm dark lentils)

2½ cups chicken stock or low-sodium chicken broth, or as needed

2½ cups water, or as needed

1 small yellow squash, cut into ½-inch dice

½ bunch Swiss chard (¾ pound), ribs removed and discarded, leaves coarsely chopped

2 tablespoons freshly squeezed lemon juice

Freshly ground black pepper

1   Pour the olive oil into a large soup pot set over medium heat. Add the onions, garlic, crushed red pepper and cilantro, along with a large pinch of salt, and cook, stirring, until the onions are softened and just barely beginning to brown, about 10 minutes.

2   Add the lentils, chicken stock and water, turn the heat to high and bring the mixture to a boil. Lower the heat and simmer until the lentils are just tender, about 30 minutes.

3   Add the yellow squash and Swiss chard and cook, stirring occasionally, until softened but still bright in color, about 5 minutes. If you would like a thinner soup, add more broth or water ½ cup at a time.

4   When the soup is the consistency you like, stir in the lemon juice and season to taste with salt and pepper.

5   Ladle the soup into bowls and serve immediately.

MAKE AHEAD The soup can be refrigerated for up to 3 days or frozen for up to 3 months. Reheat gently, adding more liquid if desired.

Creamy Roasted Carrot Soup with Pine Nut + Caper Topping

❝ One of my favorite soups is carrot ginger, but until recently, it was definitely not one of my favorite soups to make. I'd screwed it up too many times. The first time I tried a recipe, I simmered the carrots in broth, then poured the hot liquid and vegetables into the blender. I put the top on and whirred. Within seconds, the orange soup had exploded out of the top and splattered all over the walls, the stove and my sweater. When I consulted Jenn Louis of Lincoln in Portland, Oregon, she had this recommendation: Use an immersion blender or, if using a regular blender, fill it only halfway, take the plug out of the lid and cover the hole with a towel so some of the steam can escape. The softened vegetables will puree to a gorgeous soupy consistency, with no geyser!

ACTIVE TIME: 30 MINUTES   TOTAL TIME: 1½ HOURS   SERVES 8

FOR THE CARROTS

2½ pounds carrots, scrubbed and sliced ¼ inch thick (about 8 cups)
3 tablespoons extra-virgin olive oil
Kosher salt

FOR THE PINE NUT + CAPER TOPPING

½ cup plus 2 tablespoons extra-virgin olive oil
½ cup roughly chopped pine nuts
2 small garlic cloves, chopped
3 tablespoons capers, dried well on paper towels
1 cup flat-leaf parsley leaves
Kosher salt

TO FINISH THE SOUP

2 tablespoons extra-virgin olive oil
1 large yellow onion, diced (about 1½ cups)
2 large garlic cloves, chopped
6 cups chicken stock or low-sodium chicken broth
Kosher salt and freshly ground black pepper

1 For the carrots, preheat the oven to 450°F. Line a baking sheet with parchment paper.

2 Put the carrots in a large bowl and toss with the olive oil and a large pinch of salt. Transfer to the prepared baking sheet, spread them out and roast, stirring occasionally until tender and very browned, 30 to 40 minutes. Remove from the oven.

3 Meanwhile, prepare the topping: Heat the olive oil in a small skillet over medium-low heat until shimmering. Add the pine nuts and garlic and cook, stirring occasionally, until the nuts are light golden brown, about 30 seconds. Add the capers and cook for another 20 seconds or so, until crisp.

4 Transfer the mixture to the bowl of a food processor, add the parsley and salt to taste and pulse to make a not-too-smooth puree. Set aside.

5 To finish the soup, heat the olive oil in a large heavy pot over medium-low heat until shimmering. Add the onions and garlic and cook, stirring occasionally, until they are softened and just barely beginning to take on color, about 5 minutes.

6 Add the chicken stock and bring to a boil, then lower the heat to a simmer. Season the soup to taste with salt and pepper. Add the roasted carrots, take the pot off the stove and place it on a heatproof surface.

7 Using an immersion blender, carefully puree the soup until completely smooth. Alternatively, transfer the soup, in batches, to a conventional blender, filling it no more than halfway. Remove the plug from the lid, to vent the blender, cover the top tightly with a kitchen towel and puree. Add water to the soup if desired for a thinner consistency. Season again to taste with salt and pepper.

8 Ladle the soup into bowls, drizzle with the caper topping and serve.

NOTE The soup can also be made by cooking the carrots in the onion and stock mixture until they're soft, for 20 to 30 minutes, then pureeing the soup. While you won't get the caramelized flavor of the roasted carrots, you will still have a great bowl of soup.

MAKE AHEAD The soup can be refrigerated for up to 3 days or frozen for up to 3 months.

---

chef tips from
jenn louis

ON ACHIEVING THE PERFECT CONSISTENCY It is easier to thin a thick soup than to thicken a thin soup. If adding liquid to thin the soup, start with a small amount, then add more if desired.

ON GETTING MORE FLAVOR FROM CARROTS Roasting vegetables rather than simmering them will concentrate their flavor.

ON CHECKING ROASTED VEGETABLES FOR DONENESS When roasting the vegetables, make sure they're soft enough that they will be able to fully puree, without leaving any firm chunks. To test them for tenderness, pierce them with a skewer.

CHEF VARIATION To make the soup even creamier without using cream, add more olive oil, fresh bread crumbs or nuts when you puree it.

butter lettuce with sweet-tart
dijon dressing, page 44

salads

butter lettuce with sweet-tart dijon dressing · 44

spicy greens caesar salad · 45

seven-green kale salad with buttermilk dressing · 47

broccoli stem, celery + pumpkin seed salad · 49

beet, tart plum + ginger salad · 51

bloody mary salad · 54

napa cabbage slaw · 55

two favorite crunchy salads · 56

jicama, asian pear + pomegranate salad · 56

snap peas with pickled shallot dressing · 58

Butter Lettuce with Sweet-Tart Dijon Dressing

chef tips from
suzanne goin

ON THE PERFECT OIL-TO-VINEGAR RATIO All vinegars have differing acidity, but almost every one (and this goes for lemon juice too) works at a 2:1 oil-to-vinegar ratio—although most people say the perfect ratio is 3:1. Red wine vinegar is the only exception. It is stronger and more acidic than other vinegars and works best at 5 tablespoons olive oil to 2 tablespoons red wine vinegar.

ON HOW TO TASTE A VINAIGRETTE Vinaigrettes can taste sharp when you try them on their own; always test them on greens. This way, you don't end up with a flabby vinaigrette that's not acidic enough. Tasted on their own, vinaigrettes should make your mouth pucker.

ON VINEGAR If you have only one vinegar, go with Sanchez Romate sherry vinegar for its deep, earthy, subtle notes. Sherry vinegar goes well with so many things.

ON HOW MUCH DRESSING TO MAKE For a properly dressed salad, count on about a tablespoon per serving.

> For every party I host, I put a gigantic wooden bowl filled with greens on the table. This means, of course, that I need to make a dressing. I usually stick to a fairly classic vinaigrette that includes Dijon mustard, honey, red wine vinegar and extra-virgin olive oil, one that I seem to recall my mother teaching me how to make during my college years. But I've come to doubt this recollection, as that would imply she'd made a salad first, and that's nearly impossible since she rarely eats greens or prepares meals. In any case, even though I'd made the vinaigrette hundreds of times, it still troubled me. I could never remember the ratio of oil to vinegar, so it would start out too tart, then slosh toward too sweet when I spooned in more honey, and on and on. So I asked fabulous Cal-Ital chef Suzanne Goin, of Lucques in Los Angeles, for the magic ratio that would give me the right results every time. I'm hoping that by writing it down in this cookbook, I'll remember it forever: a 2:1 ratio of oil to vinegar for almost all vinegars; if it's red wine vinegar, use closer to 3:1.

TOTAL TIME: 15 MINUTES   SERVES 8

1 small garlic clove, minced
2 teaspoons Dijon mustard
1 tablespoon honey
2 tablespoons red wine vinegar
½ teaspoon kosher salt
5 tablespoons extra-virgin olive oil
2 heads butter lettuce, separated into leaves, washed, dried and torn

1 Put the garlic, mustard, honey, vinegar and salt in a bowl and whisk to thoroughly combine. While whisking, very slowly drizzle in the olive oil to form a thick, emulsified dressing. (Alternatively, put all of the dressing ingredients in a small jar, cover with the lid and shake vigorously.)
2 Put the lettuce in a serving bowl, pour the dressing evenly over it and toss to coat. Serve immediately.

MAKE AHEAD The dressing can be refrigerated for up to 1 week. The lettuce can be washed, dried, rolled in paper towels and stored in a plastic bag in the refrigerator for up to 3 days.

Spicy Greens Caesar Salad

❝ When my husband, Barclay, gets home late from work and hasn't had dinner, he sometimes throws together a super-pungent Caesar salad. It's a holdover from his bachelor days that he makes with a heavy dose of smashed garlic, a boatload of anchovies and a storm of cheese. It's incredibly delicious. For his birthday one year, I wanted to have it on the menu, but I worried that his version would overwhelm our friends! So I searched for an easy, less pungent recipe. One developed by *Food & Wine*'s former test kitchen supervisor, Marcia Kiesel, which is a- *F&W* staff favorite, was the perfect model. The dressing all comes together in the blender (and, like Barclay's, it doesn't have raw eggs). It's strong enough to please die-hard anchovy and garlic fans but mild enough to serve on a buffet without fear of it dominating.

TOTAL TIME: 15 MINUTES   SERVES 8

2 garlic cloves
6 anchovy fillets, drained and chopped
3 tablespoons freshly squeezed lemon juice
2 teaspoons Dijon mustard
½ cup mayonnaise
½ cup olive oil
¼ cup freshly grated Parmesan cheese
Kosher salt and freshly ground black pepper
2 pounds spicy greens, such as mustard or dandelion greens,
    torn into bite-size pieces (about 8 cups)

1 Turn your food processor on, drop the garlic cloves through the feed tube and process until finely chopped. Add the anchovies, lemon juice, mustard and mayonnaise and process until smooth. With the machine on, slowly pour in the olive oil. Transfer the dressing to a large bowl, stir in the Parmesan and season to taste with salt and pepper.

2 Add the greens to the bowl and toss to coat. Serve immediately.

MAKE AHEAD The dressing can be refrigerated for up to 1 day. The greens can be washed, dried, rolled in paper towels and stored in a plastic bag in the refrigerator for up to 3 days.

Seven-Green Kale Salad with Buttermilk Dressing

66 In the course of becoming a better cook, I also learned to make my food prettier. My chef coaches reminded me over and over that we eat with our eyes before we take the first bite. Inspired by this, I took a rather simple kale salad with apples and nuts and made it more beautiful by including as many shades of green as I could. The result has vegetables, herbs and fruits that range from hunter green to chartreuse—it's a snapshot of some of nature's most glorious hues. For the dressing, I opted for creamy buttermilk because I love the tang that it brings. But the recipe only uses half a cup of buttermilk, and I had to buy a quart. Curious as to what I could do with the leftover buttermilk, I asked Sean Brock, the visionary chef of Husk and McCrady's in Charleston, South Carolina, who provided the clever ideas listed on page 48.

TOTAL TIME: 25 MINUTES   SERVES 8

FOR THE DRESSING
½ cup buttermilk
½ cup sour cream
2 tablespoons white wine vinegar
1 garlic clove, minced
½ teaspoon kosher salt
½ teaspoon freshly ground black pepper

FOR THE SALAD
2 pounds Tuscan kale (also called dinosaur or Lacinato kale), stems removed and discarded
¼ cup olive oil
1 teaspoon kosher salt
2 green apples, cored and finely diced
1 large English cucumber, finely diced
½ cup *each* finely chopped dill, flat-leaf parsley, mint and basil
1 cup lightly toasted pine nuts (see Note)

1 Whisk together all of the dressing ingredients in a small bowl.
2 Working with a handful of leaves at a time, stack the kale leaves and cut them crosswise into thin strips.
3 Put the shredded kale in a large salad bowl, drizzle over the olive

oil and sprinkle with the salt. Using your hands, massage the kale with the olive oil and salt so that it wilts a bit. Add the apples, cucumber and herbs, then add the dressing and toss well. Scatter the pine nuts on top and serve immediately.

NOTE Toast the pine nuts in a small skillet over medium-low heat, shaking the pan occasionally, until golden brown, about 5 minutes. Transfer the nuts to a plate to cool.

MAKE AHEAD The dressing can be refrigerated for up to 1 day. Most of the salad components can be prepped and stored separately in the refrigerator for up to a day. Don't cut the apples ahead, though, or they will turn brown quickly.

WHY DIDN'T I THINK OF THAT?
MORE RECIPE IDEAS FROM SEAN BROCK

- Look at buttermilk the way most people look at yogurt—use it in any dish that needs a little acid and dairy to balance it. Replacing the milk in any recipe with buttermilk will add much more character.
- Try making homemade ricotta with buttermilk!
- My Mother's Chicken + Dumplings: Simmer a whole chicken in water and pull the meat off the bones (discard the bones). Mix flour and buttermilk to make the dumplings and poach them in the pot with the chicken and broth.
- Season buttermilk with salt and allow it to sit out on the counter for a couple of days. The buttermilk will ferment and take on a very sour note, adding another layer of complexity. It is amazing served ice-cold with raw seafood.

Broccoli Stem, Celery + Pumpkin Seed Salad

66 Wasting food is one of my pet peeves. I hate tossing scraps when they could be the beginnings of other great meals. Lots of star chefs agree—Rene Redzepi of Noma in Copenhagen, for example, is a proponent of "trash cooking," finding potential in parts of ingredients that most people throw out, like scallion roots or year-old beets. I made it my mission one day to rescue broccoli stems, so often discarded, and turn them into a salad. After the first bite, I realized why some people think broccoli stems aren't fit for consumption: the fibrous outer skin was really tough! So the next time I made the dish, I peeled away the skin, revealing the sweet, crunchy inner core. I combined the stems with celery and pumpkin seeds for a hearty winter salad. I roasted the florets and sprinkled them with a mix of smoky pimentón and salt for a separate side dish.

TOTAL TIME: 25 MINUTES   SERVES 6

2 tablespoons white wine vinegar

1 tablespoon honey

3 tablespoons extra-virgin olive oil

¼ cup plain whole-milk Greek yogurt

½ teaspoon kosher salt

½ teaspoon freshly ground black pepper

Stems from 6 heads broccoli, tough ends removed, outer layer peeled

6 large celery stalks, sliced on the bias (2 cups), plus ¼ cup roughly chopped celery leaves

½ cup toasted pumpkin seeds (see Note)

¼ cup roughly chopped flat-leaf parsley

1 Whisk together the vinegar, honey, olive oil, yogurt, salt and pepper in a large salad bowl. Set aside.

2 Slice the broccoli stems lengthwise in half, then cut on the bias into thin slices. You should have about 4 cups.

3 Add the broccoli stems to the bowl with the dressing, then add the celery, celery leaves, pumpkin seeds and parsley and toss to combine. Serve immediately.

NOTE Toast the pumpkin seeds in a small skillet over medium heat until lightly browned, about 5 minutes. Transfer to a plate to cool.

Beet, Tart Plum + Ginger Salad

" If you wrap beets in aluminum foil to roast them, how are you supposed to tell when they're done? That was my question when I pulled back the foil swaddling some gorgeous beets and realized that I had seriously overcooked them. They were burn victims, with splotches of brown. The answer is simple, said Jean-Georges Vongerichten, whose recipe provided the basis for this beet and plum salad: just pierce the foil with a thin knife to check the beets (and then pull some of the foil over to cover the tiny hole), and take them out when the flesh is tender. I serve the beets warm with plums of the same color and a light, subtle ginger dressing.

ACTIVE TIME: 20 MINUTES   TOTAL TIME: 2 HOURS   SERVES 8

4 large red or yellow beets (about 3 pounds), scrubbed and trimmed
¼ cup extra-virgin olive oil
3 tablespoons sherry vinegar, or more to taste
1 tablespoon grated (preferably on a Microplane) peeled ginger
½ teaspoon kosher salt, or more to taste
2 red or yellow plums (the same color as the beets), pitted and sliced into half-moons (about 2 cups)
2 scallions, thinly sliced

1 Preheat the oven to 400°F.

2 Put the beets in the center of a large piece of foil on a baking sheet, drizzle a tablespoon of water on the beets and wrap them in the foil, forming a tight package. Roast the beets until a paring knife can be inserted into a beet through the foil without any resistance, 1 to 1½ hours (start checking after 45 minutes). Remove the beets from the oven and let them cool slightly. Unwrap.

3 When the beets are just cool enough to handle, use a paper towel to rub off their skins. Trim the stem and root ends. Transfer the beets to a cutting board covered with a piece of parchment paper (to prevent it from staining) and cut them into wedges that are the same size as the plums (see Note). To prevent your hands from getting stained with beet juice, use a fork in one hand to hold the beets and slice with the other hand.

4 Whisk together the oil, vinegar, ginger and salt in a large bowl. Using the parchment paper to help you, transfer the warm beets to the bowl and toss gently to coat. Season with more vinegar or salt if needed.

5 Transfer the beets to a platter and scatter the plums and scallions on top. Give the salad one final sprinkle of salt and serve immediately.

chef tips from
jean-georges vongerichten

ON CUTTING BEETS Cover your cutting board with parchment paper to prevent it from getting stained. Once the beets are chopped, you can just pick up the parchment and slide them into the bowl without staining your hands.

ON DRESSING THE BEETS Dress the beets while they're warm. As with potato salad, they will absorb so much more flavor. Once dressed, the salad can sit for a while, but only at room temperature—not in the refrigerator; the refrigerator changes the flavor too much. You can serve the salad warm or at room temperature.

ON DRESSING THE PLUMS The plums will not hold up in the dressing for longer than about an hour.

ON OTHER WAYS TO USE BEETS Juice them! Add soda water to the juice to serve as a refreshing drink. Or reduce the juice to a syrup, whisk in olive oil and season with salt. Use as a sauce or a dressing.

ON USING BEET GREENS Always keep the beet greens. You can boil them until they're tender and use them in a ravioli filling. Or, for a side dish, chop the greens, blanch them and dress them with olive oil, balsamic vinegar, salt and pepper. Serve with ricotta.

ON USING GINGER PEELS I peel ginger using a paring knife. Then I dry the peels low and slow in the oven, pulverize them with salt and sugar and use the mixture to rim the glass for a ginger margarita!

ON THE ELEMENTS OF A PERFECT DISH It should have sweetness, spiciness, crunch and acidity. Food has to pop, and the second bite has to be as exciting as the first.

ON A COOKING SHORTCUT You can also boil the beets in salted water, and leave some of the stems on when you cut them—the stems will flavor the cooking water. This method is faster than roasting.

Bloody Mary Salad

66 Hard-core foodies might be reluctant to serve tomatoes in winter, when they are out of season, but I have found the perfect way to use the cherry tomatoes that are available all year long: I re-create the flavors of a Bloody Mary in a salad by spiking the tomatoes with a tangy, spicy dressing with hits of horseradish and Tabasco. Once I hunted down fresh horseradish, which is in season in the winter, and microplaned it into the dressing. But the fresh-from-the-farm root was too mild and I switched to jarred horseradish. Perfectly appropriate for this out-of-season salad.

TOTAL TIME: 15 MINUTES   SERVES 4

¼ cup plain whole-milk Greek yogurt
½ teaspoon kosher salt
1 tablespoon prepared horseradish
1 tablespoon white wine vinegar
Tabasco sauce to taste
1 pound cherry tomatoes, halved
4 large celery stalks, thinly sliced on the bias
¼ cup Spanish green olives, pitted and roughly chopped

1 Whisk together the yogurt, salt, horseradish and vinegar in a small bowl. Add as much Tabasco as you like.
2 Place the tomatoes on a platter and scatter the celery and olives on top. Drizzle with the dressing and serve immediately.

MAKE AHEAD The dressing can be refrigerated for up to 3 days.

Napa Cabbage Slaw

"Chefs have become obsessed with cabbage—and if chefs are obsessed, then I am too. I now want to know everything about it, including the easiest way to make it taste great. I gave this challenge to Julia Turshen, my collaborator on the book, and she came back with this easy, refreshing side dish. All it takes is thinly slicing cabbage and scallions, finely chopping mint and cilantro and then tossing them together with olive oil and lime juice. Now that I've embraced this slaw, I want to put it on everything—Korean meat loaf (see page 148), sliders (see page 27) and sandwiches.

TOTAL TIME: 20 MINUTES   SERVES 8

1½ pounds napa cabbage, cored and very thinly sliced
   (about 8 cups)
6 scallions, thinly sliced on the bias
½ cup lightly packed mint leaves, finely chopped
½ cup lightly packed cilantro leaves, finely chopped
¼ cup olive oil
3 tablespoons freshly squeezed lime juice
1 teaspoon kosher salt

Put all the ingredients in a large bowl and toss well to combine. Let the slaw sit for at least 10 minutes before serving.

MAKE AHEAD The slaw can be refrigerated for up to 4 hours. Be sure to toss it again before serving.

Two Favorite Crunchy Salads

❝ Tired of my usual roster of salads, I asked Tina Ujlaki, *Food &Wine*'s executive food editor, for a recipe that would break up the greens monotony. Her suggestion was a chopped vegetable salad from chef Deborah Madison, which opened up a whole new world of chunky salads. I first made the salad with the ingredients Deborah suggested: cauliflower, broccoflower, olives and capers. But it dawned on me that this would work with a vast range of chopped raw, seasonal, crunchy vegetables, fruits and seeds. I began experimenting, and I'm sharing my two favorites with you.

Jicama, Asian Pear + Pomegranate Salad

TOTAL TIME: 25 MINUTES   SERVES 8

¼ cup freshly squeezed lemon juice
⅓ cup extra-virgin olive oil
½ teaspoon kosher salt
1 large jicama, peeled and cut into ½-inch dice (4 cups)
1 large Asian pear (or 2 green apples), cored and very thinly sliced
1 cup pomegranate seeds (from ½ large pomegranate)
Freshly ground black pepper

Whisk together the lemon juice, olive oil and salt in a large bowl. Add the jicama and pear and toss to coat. Transfer the salad to a serving bowl, scatter the pomegranate seeds on top and sprinkle with pepper. Serve immediately.

NOTES You may need to go over the jicama with a peeler twice to remove every bit of the thick, tough skin. Use chilled ingredients to ensure a supercrisp and refreshing salad.
MAKE AHEAD The salad can be refrigerated for up to 1 day.

Snap Peas with Pickled Shallot Dressing

TOTAL TIME: 30 MINUTES   SERVES 8

....

⅓ cup freshly squeezed lemon juice
1 teaspoon kosher salt, plus more to taste
1 teaspoon sugar
3 large shallots, thinly sliced (½ cup)
1½ pounds (about 8 cups) snap peas, ends trimmed
½ cup extra-virgin olive oil
Small handful of pea flowers (optional)
Freshly ground black pepper

1 Whisk together the lemon juice, salt and sugar in a small bowl. Stir in the shallots and let them sit, stirring occasionally, until they're wilted and taste pickled, about 20 minutes.

2 Meanwhile, thinly slice the snap peas on the bias. Put them in a large bowl.

3 Using a slotted spoon, transfer the shallots to the bowl with the snap peas, leaving their pickling liquid in the small bowl. Slowly whisk the olive oil into the pickling liquid to make an emulsified dressing.

4 Pour the dressing over the snap peas, add the pea flowers, if you have them, and toss to combine. Season the salad to taste with more salt and with pepper. Serve immediately.

roasted winter vegetables with
miso vinaigrette, page 62

vegetables

Roasted Winter Vegetables with Miso Vinaigrette

> A sports coach for my son, William, once told me that the sign of a great player is consistency. If a kid could hit the ball the same way time and again, he said, he could be a star. The same goes for cooking. Great restaurant chefs make the same dish the exact same way night after night. I now aspire to this in my cooking.

In winter, I get a lot of practice making roasted vegetables. My daughter and I routinely go "bin diving"—we open the fridge's produce bin and take out all the wounded vegetables, dice them, toss them with olive oil and roast them. Sometimes they come out perfectly—the flavors intensified and delicious. But sometimes they burn on the bottom and are still raw on the top. Determined to become more consistent, I asked April Bloomfield to be my vegetable-roasting coach. She had two excellent recommendations: Be sure to cut the vegetables into the right size so they cook at the same time. For example, carrots and Brussels sprouts won't cook at the same rate, so carrots need to be cut smaller to cook in the same amount of time or similar as the less-dense Brussels sprouts. And stir the vegetables occasionally as they roast, for even cooking.

ACTIVE TIME: 35 MINUTES   TOTAL TIME: 1 HOUR + 25 MINUTES
SERVES 8

....

4 pounds winter vegetables, peeled and/or trimmed as necessary and cut into 1-inch pieces (about 8 cups); I like a combination of butternut squash, white and sweet potatoes, Brussels sprouts and parsnips, but use whatever you have on hand

3 tablespoons extra-virgin olive oil

1 teaspoon kosher salt

2 teaspoons Asian sesame oil

1/4 cup rice vinegar

3 tablespoons white miso

1 tablespoon soy sauce

2 tablespoons honey

2 tablespoons toasted sesame seeds

3 scallions, thinly sliced

1 Position the racks in the upper and lower thirds of the oven and preheat the oven to 400°F. Line two rimmed baking sheets with parchment paper.

2 Put the vegetables in a large bowl and toss with the olive oil and salt. Divide the vegetables evenly between the two baking sheets, spread them out and roast, stirring occasionally, until tender and very browned, 30 to 40 minutes. Switch and rotate the baking sheets halfway through cooking.

3 Meanwhile, put the sesame oil, rice vinegar, miso, soy sauce and honey in a small bowl and whisk together.

4 Remove the vegetables from the oven and transfer to a serving bowl. Immediately toss with the miso vinaigrette. Scatter the sesame seeds and scallions on top and serve.

MAKE AHEAD The dressing can be refrigerated for up to 1 week. Bring to room temperature before tossing with the vegetables.

WHY DIDN'T I THINK OF THAT?
MORE RECIPE IDEAS FROM APRIL BLOOMFIELD

- Roast wedges of pumpkin seasoned with a paste made of garlic, fresh marjoram, cinnamon, salt and olive oil.
- Celery root is underrated! Season chunks of it with olive oil, ground chile, garlic and salt and roast until tender.
- Fennel is wonderful seasoned with ground fennel seeds, chopped fennel fronds, garlic, salt and olive oil.
- For even simpler roast fennel, place slices on a baking sheet lined with parchment paper, splash with a little water and olive oil and cover with foil. Roast until tender, then remove the foil and continue to roast, turning occasionally, until caramelized.

chef tips from
april bloomfield

ON HOW TO CUT THE VEGETABLES If you are roasting different kinds of vegetables on the same tray at the same time, cut them according to their cooking times. For example, a thinly sliced onion will roast much faster than a large wedge of sweet potato. So, if you're doing them together, cut the sweet potato into smaller pieces and the onion into slightly larger ones.

ON PREPPING THE VEGETABLES Always toss vegetables with olive oil before roasting. This is especially important for tougher vegetables like pumpkin, fennel and celery root.

Quickest Cucumber Kimchi

> Taking my cue from the brilliant cross-cultural pollinator chef David Chang of Momofuku, I planned on serving kimchi at a July 4th lunch. But when it came time to lay out the spread on the picnic table, the kimchi didn't make it. The fish sauce had overpowered my dish. I wanted to blame the brand of fish sauce—maybe my cheap supermarket version wasn't good. But David set me straight.

He said that fish sauces, made from salted fermented fish, like anchovies, are essentially all the same. It's more likely I was a little too generous with my fish sauce pour. Used sparingly, fish sauce adds an umami flavor. Overused, it leads directly to the trash. I've made this dish many times since with the right amount of fish sauce, and it's always popular.

TOTAL TIME: 20 MINUTES   SERVES 8

2 teaspoons kosher salt, or more to taste

1 tablespoon plus 2 teaspoons sugar, or more to taste

2 pounds Kirby cucumbers, thinly sliced

1 small carrot, peeled and thinly sliced

¼ small white onion, thinly sliced

One 1-inch piece of ginger, peeled and chopped

2 garlic cloves

2 scallions, cut into 1-inch pieces

1 tablespoon fish sauce

1 tablespoon soy sauce

1 tablespoon *gochugaru* (Korean red chile flakes; see Note)

1 Stir the salt and 2 teaspoons of the sugar together in a small bowl. Put the cucumbers, carrot and onion on a large rimmed baking sheet and toss with the salt and sugar. Let sit while you make the dressing.

2 Combine the remaining 1 tablespoon sugar, the ginger, garlic, scallions, fish sauce and soy sauce in a food processor and puree into a paste. Season to taste with more salt or sugar if you think it needs it.

3 Transfer the cucumbers and carrots to a large bowl and add the *gochugaru.* Toss with the dressing to coat and serve.

NOTE It's worth seeking out the *gochugaru*, which has a distinctive flavor. You can find it at Asian markets or online. Or see "On Spice" in the Chef Tips on the following page.

chef tips from **david chang**

ON CHOPPING When you're chopping, use the whole blade of your knife and slice with a clean motion. If you hear "bang, bang, bang," you know you're listening to someone who doesn't know how to chop properly. Start with the tip and slice long. It's like wheel alignment.

ON SLICING CUCUMBERS FOR KIMCHI

- Don't worry too much about cutting perfectly. With kimchi, being inexact is a good thing.
- When you get to the end of the cucumber and there's a little left, cut off a bit from the bottom side so you can stand the final chunk upright and it won't roll. That way, you won't risk cutting your fingers. People won't notice a little bit of green missing, and it's better than missing a bit of your finger!

ON CHOPPING GINGER I like to square off a chunk of ginger before cutting it. Then I cut it into thin slices, cut the slices into long sticks and cut the sticks into small dice. To make it really fine, I go through that pile a few times.

ON SUGAR I find that sometimes kimchi can be so salty that it needs sugar to balance it out—a 50–50 mixture of salt and sugar works perfectly.

ON SEASONING I know it may look ridiculous to season from up high, but it distributes the seasoning well, so it doesn't all land on one piece of cucumber. And it makes you look like you know what you're doing! Taste the cucumbers as you go to make sure they're seasoned properly. They shouldn't taste too strong.

ON SPICE If you can't find *gochugaru* (Korean chile flakes), you can use Sriracha. The simplest way to make kimchi is to take the cucumbers tossed with salt and sugar and dress them with Sriracha—that's it! Maybe add a tiny bit of vinegar.

ON OTHER USES FOR KIMCHI DRESSING It's assertive and intense, so it's a great marinade for meat too. You can also use it to make different kinds of kimchi, such as napa cabbage or turnip. You can cut napa cabbage into small pieces and toss it with the dressing, and it's ready immediately.

Green Beans with Arugula + Lemon Pesto

66 Whenever I plan a party, I think through the menu, balancing flavors, considering prep time and trying to hit a high vegetable-to-meat ratio. I usually aim for four or five make-ahead dishes and only one that will need last-minute attention. Green beans with pesto is perfect to make ahead—unless you ruin the beans, as I did the first time I attempted this. I blanched the beans in boiling salted water as directed, then put them in an ice bath to stop the cooking and set them aside. When I was ready to serve dinner, I drained the beans and tossed them with the delicious arugula pesto I'd prepared earlier in the day. The beans were crunchy and perfectly cooked but they somehow seemed wet. I asked Napa Valley chef Maria Sinskey of Robert Sinskey Vineyards, whose recipe had inspired mine, what could have gone wrong. She explained that you need to "shock" the beans and then remove them from the water as soon as they've cooled. If they sit in the water, they'll get waterlogged.

Timing is everything. And with the right timing, this is indeed a great make-ahead dish.

TOTAL TIME: 25 MINUTES   SERVES 8 TO 10

½ cup lightly toasted pine nuts (see Note)
2 small garlic cloves, roughly chopped
Kosher salt
4 lightly packed cups baby arugula (3½ ounces)
1 cup extra-virgin olive oil
2 tablespoons finely grated lemon zest (from 3 lemons), plus more
    for garnish
2 tablespoons freshly squeezed lemon juice, or to taste
3 pounds green beans, ends trimmed
½ cup freshly grated Pecorino cheese
Freshly ground black pepper

1 Put the pine nuts in the bowl of a food processor, add the garlic and a pinch of salt and pulse until finely chopped. Add the arugula and pulse until finely chopped. With the machine on, slowly drizzle in the olive oil and process until the pesto is smooth. Stir in the lemon zest and then the juice a little at a time, tasting as you go. Set the pesto aside.

2 Bring a very large pot of water to a boil. Add enough salt to the boiling water to make it taste like the ocean. Taste the water! Seriously.

This is your opportunity to season the green beans from the inside out. Fill a large bowl with ice and water.

3 Add the green beans to the boiling water and cook until just tender, 1 to 3 minutes, depending on the freshness and size of the beans. (Depending on the size of your pot, you may need to blanch the beans in batches. Use tongs to transfer them to the ice bath so you can reuse the boiling water.) Drain the beans and immediately plunge them into the ice water to stop the cooking. As soon as the beans are cool, drain them, then dry them thoroughly on paper towels.

4 Put the beans in a large serving bowl and add the pesto and half of the Pecorino, tossing to coat. Scatter the remaining cheese on top, sprinkle with lemon zest and pepper and serve immediately.

NOTE Toast the pine nuts in a small skillet over medium-low heat, shaking the pan occasionally, until golden brown, about 5 minutes. Transfer the nuts to a plate to cool.

MAKE AHEAD The blanched green beans can be wrapped in paper towels and stored in a resealable bag in the refrigerator for up to 2 days.

chef tips from **maria sinskey**

ON BLANCHING BEANS The perfect way to cook green beans is to blanch them in well-salted water until just tender (the thicker the beans, the longer they will take).

ON CHILLING BEANS "Shock" blanched beans in ice water just until thoroughly chilled, then drain well.

ON HOW MUCH OIL TO ADD TO PESTO Pesto should always taste more of the herbs than the oil. To get the right ratio, slowly add the oil to the herbs while the processor is running.

ON WHICH OIL TO USE FOR PESTO Don't use an olive oil that has too powerful a flavor, or you risk masking the delicate flavors of the herbs.

ON FIXING A BROKEN PESTO If the pesto breaks (separates), you've added too much oil. To repair it, transfer it to a bowl, add more fresh herbs to the food processor and process, slowly adding the broken pesto until you get the desired consistency.

ON ADDING BRIGHTNESS TO PESTO Add acid at the end, a few drops at a time, until there is a spark of brightness.

Roasted Brussels Sprouts with Caper-Raisin Sauce

" This caper-raisin puree is one of the tastiest and easiest but ugliest sauces I've ever poured out of the blender. It's based on a recipe from the amazingly talented chef Jean-Georges Vongerichten of Jean-Georges in New York City. The fact that it looks unappetizing is not a problem I can correct, but it is one that I can ignore because it's just so good on everything from roasted Brussels sprouts to seared cauliflower steaks.

ACTIVE TIME: 20 MINUTES   TOTAL TIME: 50 MINUTES   SERVES 8

2 pounds Brussels sprouts, trimmed and halved
¼ cup olive oil
Kosher salt
½ cup capers, rinsed and drained
½ cup raisins
4 tablespoons (½ stick) unsalted butter
1 cup water
2½ tablespoons sherry vinegar
Small handful of flat-leaf parsley leaves, finely chopped

1   Preheat the oven to 400°F. Line a rimmed baking sheet with foil.
2   Put the Brussels sprouts on the baking sheet, toss with the olive oil and season liberally with salt. Roast, stirring once or twice, until softened and browned in spots, about 30 minutes.
3   Meanwhile, put the capers, raisins, butter and water in a small saucepan and bring to a boil. Turn the heat to medium-low and simmer until the raisins are plump, about 5 minutes.
4   Carefully transfer the raisin mixture to a blender, add the vinegar and blend until smooth. Season the sauce to taste with salt and pour it into a small bowl.
5   Transfer the Brussels sprouts to a serving bowl and scatter the parsley on top. Serve the warm sauce alongside for drizzling.

MAKE AHEAD The sauce can be refrigerated for up to 1 week. Reheat gently before serving.

Blistered Tomatoes, Fairy Tale Eggplant + Corn

❝ Shopping can be as important a skill as cooking: this is something I've learned in my quest to become a better cook. Since I'd never gotten eggplant shopping quite right, I was doomed to cook with seedy, bitter eggplant. This was frustrating because after reading Yotam Ottolenghi's cookbook *Plenty*, I really wanted to make his recipes and experiment with my own. After discussing my issue with Tina Ujlaki, *F&W*'s executive food editor, she brought back the most delicate Fairy Tale eggplant from the greenmarket. They were slender, tiny, pale purple-and-white specimens with few seeds and thin skins, and they needed almost no cooking. I sautéed them, then blistered some tomatoes in a pan and added them both to fresh-cut corn kernels. The dish was so good that it convinced me to always be on the lookout for slender eggplant. The choice can make the difference between delicious and disaster. To further my eggplant education, I consulted Yotam. His tips are at left.

chef tips from yotam ottolenghi

ON CHOOSING THE BEST EGGPLANT To make sure your eggplant is not full of seeds or cottony, choose ones that have a firm, smooth, glossy skin, with bright green tops.

ON SEASONING EGGPLANT Eggplant can take a lot of seasoning—don't hold back.

ON GETTING EGGPLANT GOLDEN BROWN Don't hold back on oil either—eggplant needs plenty if you want it to turn nice and golden brown.

ON ROASTING EGGPLANT Brush the eggplant with tons of olive oil, season with a fair amount of salt and put it straight into a hot oven to roast until properly browned, about 30 minutes.

TOTAL TIME: 40 MINUTES   SERVES 8

Olive oil, for frying
1½ pounds Fairy Tale or Japanese eggplant, thinly sliced into rounds, ends discarded,
4 cups (1½ pounds) cherry tomatoes
Kernels from 4 ears sweet corn
¼ cup coarsely chopped flat-leaf parsley
Kosher salt and freshly ground black pepper

1 Heat ¼ cup olive oil in a large cast-iron skillet over medium-high heat. When the oil just barely begins to smoke, add enough eggplant to make a single layer and cook, stirring occasionally, until crisp and golden brown, about 5 minutes. Transfer the eggplant to a large bowl and repeat in batches, adding more oil as needed, until you've cooked all of the eggplant.

2 Discard the oil remaining in the pan, add the cherry tomatoes and cook, shaking the skillet occasionally, until they are charred in spots, about 8 minutes. Transfer the tomatoes to the bowl with the eggplant.

3 Add the corn kernels and parsley to the bowl and toss to combine. Season to taste with salt and pepper. Serve immediately, or let cool and serve at room temperature.

Spiced Creamed Spinach

66 For a long-ago Thanksgiving dinner at my parents' apartment, I was in charge of making the spinach. I had never cooked fresh spinach before—I grew up eating "square spinach," the kind that came in a frozen block. But it seemed simple enough: wash, then cook. My older cousin Pat was the self-appointed taster. She took one bite, spit it out and then asked, "How many times did you wash the spinach?" It was horribly gritty. She patiently explained that "rinsing" isn't enough to get the sand out. So we washed the wilted mess until there were about two handfuls of spinach left, and Pat added what seemed like a pint of cream. It was enough for about three people, which was exactly the number willing to try the rescued dish.

Chef Dan Barber, of Blue Hill at Stone Barns, has the answer on this one: soak then swirl the greens in a sink full of cold water, then pull the greens out, leaving the grit behind, and dry them on paper towels.

TOTAL TIME: 20 MINUTES   SERVES 8

3 tablespoons canola oil

6 small garlic cloves, minced

2 tablespoons minced peeled ginger

$1/2$ teaspoon crushed red pepper

2 teaspoons ground coriander

3 pounds baby spinach, well rinsed and dried

Kosher salt

$3/4$ cup sour cream

$1/4$ cup finely chopped cilantro, for garnish

1 Heat the canola oil in a large heavy pot over medium-high heat until shimmering. Add the garlic, ginger, crushed red pepper and coriander and cook, stirring, until the garlic and ginger are softened and the mixture is wonderfully fragrant, just a minute or so.

2 Add the spinach in large handfuls and cook, stirring occasionally, until all of the spinach is wilted, about 5 minutes. Season the spinach with a couple of large pinches of salt, then cook until it is very tender, about 5 minutes. Transfer the spinach to a colander to drain.

3 Return the drained spinach to the pot and stir in the sour cream. Let the mixture cook until bubbles form around the edges of the pot and the spinach is creamy, about 3 minutes.

4 Season to taste with additional salt if needed. Serve hot, garnished with the chopped cilantro.

WHY DIDN'T I THINK OF THAT?
ANOTHER RECIPE IDEA FROM DAN BARBER

- Make a spinach sauce: Sauté minced shallots in brown butter (add grapeseed oil to prevent the butter from burning), then cook the spinach until tender and puree it with water and a little chopped mint. It's somewhere between a puree and a sauce, and it's delicious with meat.
- The advice I give my cooks: If the spinach is flat and flimsy, you need to cook it for a long time to break it down and release the sugars. If the spinach is textured and thick (like the popular Bloomsdale variety), a quick sauté—barely a wilt—is enough to bring out the sweetness.

chef tips from
dan barber

ON WASHING SPINACH
The best way to clean fresh spinach and other sandy greens is to soak, swirl and lift. Fill a large sink with very cold water, add the greens (being careful not to overcrowd them) and swirl the water to separate the grit from the greens, then lift the greens out and place them on paper towels to dry. You may need to repeat this process twice for especially dirty leaves. Do not drain the water before removing the greens, or the grit settled on the bottom of the sink will become part of the salad.

ON "SPINACH TEETH"
Perfectly cooked spinach can sometimes taste "squeaky." That is a sign of low levels of calcium in the soil. Sweet spinach, on the other hand, is an indication that the soil it was grown in was well cared for and mineralized.

Asparagus with Gribiche Vinaigrette

❝ I cooked only one entire meal for my father before he died, and I ruined a part of it. I wasn't much of a cook at the time, and his expectations weren't too high. I was mostly excited to have my father, with the rest of my family, come to my new apartment to see how the decorating had turned out. He and I shared a love of architecture and he'd helped me design the space. In accordance with my skills, I planned a simple meal. I cooked fish and steamed some very skinny asparagus. He took one bite of asparagus and asked if I'd forgotten to cook them. I explained that they were perfect; *exactly* the way they were supposed to be. What I remember, and regret, is my slightly obnoxious, "Don't you know anything about food today?" tone. Particularly since I had a nagging suspicion he was right.

Iconic chef and vegetable whisperer Alice Waters recently confirmed my hunch. First she explained that she believes asparagus is better when it is fat and juicy and fully cooked, not crunchy (but also "not droopy the way the French like it"). The gribiche vinaigrette, with chopped capers and cornichons, is something I added recently to make the dish a bit more interesting.

TOTAL TIME: 25 MINUTES   SERVES 8

Kosher salt

3 bunches of thick asparagus (about 4 dozen spears), tough ends discarded

1 tablespoon Dijon mustard

3 tablespoons freshly squeezed lemon juice

½ cup extra-virgin olive oil

½ teaspoon freshly ground black pepper

2 tablespoons capers, finely chopped

8 cornichons, finely chopped

2 large hard-boiled eggs, very finely chopped

1 Bring a large pot of water to a boil and season generously with salt.

2 Add 1 bunch of asparagus to the boiling water and cook until bright green and tender, about 3 minutes (start checking with a paring knife after 2 minutes). Using tongs, immediately transfer the asparagus to a paper-towel-lined baking sheet to cool. Repeat with the remaining asparagus, in two batches. Transfer the asparagus to a platter and set it aside.

3 Put the mustard and lemon juice in a small bowl and whisk together. While whisking, slowly drizzle in the olive oil, then whisk in the pepper and ½ teaspoon salt. Stir in the capers, cornichons and eggs.

4 Spoon the dressing over the asparagus and serve immediately.

chef tips from **alice waters**

ON CHOOSING THE BEST ASPARAGUS I look for something that has not been sitting around. Go to the farmers' market and get asparagus that has just been picked that day. The first of the year are the best stalks—asparagus is absolutely a springtime vegetable, with a relatively short life, only April and May. Avoid asparagus with bottom stems that are sealed and a little brown.

ON FAT VERSUS THIN ASPARAGUS I like juicy, fat asparagus with really tight ends—unless they're thin wild asparagus, like the ones I had in Provence, but that's another story. . . .

ON PREPPING ASPARAGUS Snap the tough ends off and put them in the compost, or use them for asparagus soup.

ON EVEN COOKING I'm very particular with size. Ensuring that all the stalks are similar in size means they will cook evenly.

ON KEEPING ASPARAGUS BRIGHT GREEN Never put too much asparagus in the pot at the same time. The water never gets hot enough again and then they just sit in warmish water. I believe that takes away from the color. And, as with green beans, be sure to use enough salt; you need salty water.

ON CHECKING FOR DONENESS Stick a knife in a stalk—it should go in gently. You're looking for something in between raw and droopy.

ON KEEPING ASPARAGUS FLAVORFUL When the asparagus is done, don't stop the cooking with cold water—that will take away from the taste. Let the asparagus cool on their own to room temperature. Never refrigerate asparagus, either before or after cooking.

ON PERFECT STALKS If you have time, peel the asparagus stalks. There is something very nice and luxurious about the texture of peeled asparagus.

WHY DIDN'T I THINK OF THAT? MORE RECIPE IDEAS FROM ALICE WATERS

- Cut asparagus very thin and use it in a pasta dish with a little bit of cream and lots of herbs and linguine, so that the pasta and the asparagus almost have the same textural feeling.
- Serve warm, not cold, asparagus with a zingy beurre blanc or a little vinaigrette with Meyer lemon.
- Sometimes asparagus comes really early in the season and truffles really late. Take advantage, and serve asparagus with a truffle vinaigrette. That's nice as a side for spring salmon.
- Cut asparagus into small pieces on the bias and add them to a little vegetable ragout with peas and artichokes and other small spring vegetables, along with lots of spring herbs.

Roasted Acorn Squash with Maple Syrup + Coriander

66 When I was growing up, we ate simple dishes cooked by our housekeeper, Linwood, most of them without any seasoning or adornment at all. One of the regular offerings was acorn squash, cut in half, roasted and finished with butter and maple syrup. So when I began, hesitantly, to cook in college, this was one of the first things I attempted. Though it is plain, the butter and maple syrup make it just a bit indulgent. Having mastered it long ago, I've played around with adding different herbs and spices over time to change it up. I'm sharing my favorite variation here with you.

ACTIVE TIME: 10 MINUTES   TOTAL TIME: 55 MINUTES   SERVES 6

3 acorn squash
Extra-virgin olive oil, for rubbing the squash
6 tablespoons (¾ stick) unsalted butter, melted
¼ cup plus 2 tablespoons pure maple syrup
1 teaspoon ground coriander
¾ teaspoon kosher salt

1   Preheat the oven to 400°F. Line a baking sheet with parchment paper.
2   Using a heavy chef's knife, carefully cut each squash lengthwise in half. Using a spoon, scoop out the seeds and the stringy interior and discard. Rub the squash halves with olive oil and place them cut side down on the prepared baking sheet.
3   Place the squash in the oven and bake until nearly tender (test with a paring knife), about 25 minutes, rotating the baking sheet halfway through baking.
4   Meanwhile, in a small bowl, stir together the butter, maple syrup, coriander and salt.
5   Remove the squash from the oven, turn them cut side up and pour the maple butter evenly into the cavities. Return the squash to the oven and bake until it is totally tender, the maple butter is absorbed and everything is slightly caramelized, about 20 minutes longer. Serve hot.

MAKE AHEAD The roasted squash can be refrigerated overnight. Reheat gently, brushing it with more butter if desired.

Charred Corn with Green Olives + Oregano

❝ Compulsive corn-buying syndrome, or CCBS: that's my self-diagnosis. Every weekend in the short corn season I buy a dozen ears whether we're having guests or not, whether I know when I'm going to serve them or not. Because of that, I need more recipes for corn than for any other vegetable. In one attempt to shake up my corn repertoire, I grilled the corn in its husks. First I peeled back the husks and removed the silks, then I pulled the husks back over the ears and put them on the grill. The corn never got brown; it simply cooked and turned starchy. Master of the grill Seamus Mullen, of Tertulia in New York City, gave me some fantastic advice: to avoid tough kernels, brine your corn! You soak the corn in the husks in salted water for a few hours before grilling, grill them in their husks, then shuck them and grill again to char the kernels. Once I got the perfect corn, I cut the charred kernels off the cob and tossed them with chopped olives and fresh oregano for a slightly surprising yet still familiar corn salad.

TOTAL TIME: 25 MINUTES + 2 TO 3 HOURS BRINING   SERVES 6 TO 8

¼ cup kosher salt, plus more for seasoning

8 ears corn in the husk

¼ cup extra-virgin olive oil, plus more for brushing

½ cup pitted Spanish green olives, roughly chopped

1 tablespoon finely chopped oregano

1 tablespoon freshly squeezed lemon juice

1　Two to 3 hours before cooking, fill a large pot or bowl with water (enough to submerge the ears of corn). Stir in the ¼ cup salt and soak the corn in the brine.

2　Prepare a charcoal grill or preheat a gas grill to high. Alternatively, set a heavy grill pan over high heat and lightly brush with oil.

3　Drain the corn and shake off the excess water. Grill in the husks, turning a few times, until the husks are lightly charred all over, about 8 minutes. Remove the corn from the grill and let cool slightly.

4　Shuck the corn. Brush each ear with olive oil and sprinkle generously with salt. Place the corn on the hot grill and cook, turning a few times, until bright yellow and charred in spots, about 6 minutes. Transfer the corn to a cutting board and let it sit until cool enough to handle.

5　Slice the kernels off the cobs and transfer them to a large bowl. Add the olives, oregano, lemon juice and the ¼ cup olive oil and toss to combine. Taste for seasoning and add more salt if you feel it needs it. Serve warm or at room temperature.

WHY DIDN'T I THINK OF THAT?
MORE RECIPE IDEAS FROM SEAMUS MULLEN

- When grilling corn, cook other vegetables directly in the coals—onions, peppers or eggplant—until charred on the outside and tender within. Let them cool, then remove and discard the charred outer layer and indulge in the sweet, tender, smoky interior. Toss with a little olive oil, lemon zest and fresh herbs.
- To achieve the same flavor in your kitchen, use the cast-iron grill pan again and char the veggies, turning frequently, until totally black on the outside and soft and tender inside.

chef tips from seamus mullen

ON SWEET SMOKY CORN
I *love* the charred flavor of grilled corn, but people tend to grill it until it's really tough and too charred. To avoid this, soak unshucked corn in salted water for a few hours before grilling. Grill the ears in the husks so that they steam for a few minutes, then shuck the corn and quickly grill over high heat for a few nice charred marks. You'll get a balance of smokiness and sweetness, and no dry kernels.

ON STOVETOP GRILLING
Use a cast-iron grill pan, rub it with a little olive oil then cook the presteamed corn until lightly charred.

ON SEASONING BRINE When you soak the corn in the salted water, add a splash of bourbon, some cloves of garlic and herbs.

Slow-Roasted Tomatoes with Crunchy Bread Crumbs

> My friend Joan makes the best slow-roasted tomatoes. She often serves them with cheese or tossed with pasta, or just on their own. I asked her for the recipe for her amazing tomatoes every summer, and every summer I tried to follow her directions without much success. Sometimes the bottoms blackened. Sometimes the tomatoes seemed too watery. Sometimes they shrank to almost nothing and the ambitions I had for them would evaporate—there weren't enough to even make a pasta sauce. So I went to Tom Colicchio, chef-owner of Craft restaurants and *Top Chef* head judge, who made roasted tomatoes for my wedding at his then-restaurant, Gramercy Tavern. His advice: use plum tomatoes, which have less moisture and therefore will reduce into perfect oven-roasted tomatoes more quickly, and crowd them on the baking sheet, to help prevent burning.

ACTIVE TIME: 20 MINUTES   TOTAL TIME: 2 HOURS   SERVES 8

....

12 ripe plum tomatoes
⅓ cup plus 3 tablespoons extra-virgin olive oil
Kosher salt
1 tablespoon finely chopped thyme
1 tablespoon finely chopped oregano
1½ tablespoons finely chopped basil
2 small garlic cloves, minced
Four ½-inch-thick slices of country bread (see Notes), lightly toasted

1 Position a rack in the upper third of the oven and preheat the oven to 400°F. Line a baking sheet with parchment paper.

2 Cut the tomatoes lengthwise in half and cut out and discard the tough bit of core from the top of each half. Put the tomato halves in a large bowl, drizzle with the 3 tablespoons of olive oil and sprinkle with a large pinch of salt and the thyme. Massage the oil, salt and thyme into the tomatoes.

3 Transfer the tomatoes, cut side up, to the prepared baking sheet, arranging them so they are touching. Roast until they are just softened and barely beginning to brown, about 45 minutes.

4 Meanwhile, put the remaining ⅓ cup olive oil in a medium bowl and stir in the oregano, basil, garlic and a large pinch of salt. Coarsely chop the toasted bread into small cubes (you should have about 3 cups diced bread). Add the bread to the olive oil mixture and toss to combine.

5 Remove the tomatoes from the oven and scatter the bread crumb mixture over them. Turn the oven temperature down to 325°F, return the baking sheet to the oven and roast until the bread crumbs are crisp and browned and the tomatoes are soft and concentrated, another 45 minutes or so. Serve hot or at room temperature.

NOTES For the bread, anything simple will do (e.g., ciabatta, sourdough or baguette).

During the last 15 minutes, you can scatter grated Parmesan or another favorite cheese on top of the tomatoes.

As long as the oven is on, I like to roast a second tray of tomatoes without the bread crumb topping. I keep them in my refrigerator and add them to bean dishes, pasta or stews; use for crostini; or serve with scrambled eggs.

MAKE AHEAD The tomatoes can be roasted up to the point of adding the bread crumbs, cooled and refrigerated for up to 1 week.

WHY DIDN'T I THINK OF THAT?
MORE RECIPE IDEAS FROM TOM COLICCHIO

Think of a roasted tomato not as a dish but as an ingredient:

- Brush a generous amount of olive oil on plain roasted tomatoes and serve them as a garnish for roasted fish or meat.
- For roasted tomato chutney, combine minced ginger and garlic, sugar and white wine vinegar in a pot and reduce by half. Chop the roasted tomatoes and stir them in.
- For roasted tomato soup, just add them to a pot with sautéed garlic and chicken stock; heat through and puree.
- In winter, when the herb garden is gone, turn to spices. A mixture of fennel seed, coriander seed, black pepper and cardamom is great for seasoning.

chef tips from **tom colicchio**

ON CHOOSING TOMATOES FOR ROASTING Any type of tomato can be roasted. They all work, but the timing will vary depending on the moisture. Plum tomatoes are drier, so they will roast faster. If you use Brandywine tomatoes that are ripe and in season, they will take longer to roast because they have a higher water content.

ON MAKING THE MOST OUT OF BAD TOMATOES If your tomatoes aren't super-ripe, roasting them will get the most flavor. It's a good way to make a better product out of an inferior tomato.

ON USING PARCHMENT PAPER Lining the baking sheet with parchment paper will help keep the tomatoes from burning and sticking and make it easier to transfer them later.

ON HOW MANY TOMATOES TO ROAST AT A TIME Crowd them on the baking sheet—they will shrink anyway, so go ahead and pile them on. This will also help prevent them from burning.

ON AVOIDING BURNT TOMATOES When roasting, a little dark around the edges is good, but if the bottoms are getting black, turn down the oven temperature, or double up and put another baking sheet underneath the first one. It will help lower the temperature of the surface the tomatoes are sitting on. If just the edges are getting black, give the tomatoes a stir to move them. The juices start to come to the center so the edges are drier and can begin to burn.

Zucchini + Yellow Squash with Parmesan Crisps

> In an effort to transform zucchini from a vegetable I loathe into one I love, I turned to a dish that I adored at ABC Kitchen in New York City. Dan Kluger, the chef at the time, talked me through the recipe: he tosses zucchini triangles with shredded cheese and olive oil and roasts them on a rack set over a baking sheet. It sounded so simple! But when I tried to replicate it, the rack became encrusted with shredded cheese (a cleanup disaster), and the baking sheet caught bits of cheese that then crinkled into black clumps.

Still, as with many failures, it wasn't a complete loss, because it led me to another, even simpler idea. I realized that with a little tweaking, I could actually create an easier version by cooking the zucchini and the cheese separately: the vegetables on a rack; the grated cheese on a baking sheet. The cheese was like a *frico*, or shredded cheese crisp, and I shattered it on top of the zucchini before serving. The resulting dish has a delightful contrast of crunchy cheese and warm, roasty zucchini. Eager to improve on my *frico*, I asked Italian cooking master Lidia Bastianich for pointers. She said that the key to a crisp, lacy *frico* is to coarsely grate a hard cheese such as Parmesan.

ACTIVE TIME: 20 MINUTES   TOTAL TIME: 40 MINUTES   SERVES 8

½ cup coarsely grated Parmesan cheese
2 pounds mixed zucchini and yellow squash, ends trimmed
¼ cup extra-virgin olive oil
½ teaspoon kosher salt

1 Preheat the oven to 375°F. Line two baking sheets with parchment paper.
2 Evenly space tablespoonfuls of the Parmesan on one of the prepared baking sheets, leaving about 4 inches between them. Spread the cheese so that each small pile becomes a thin round about 3 inches in diameter. Bake until the cheese melts and turns golden, about 8 minutes. Remove the baking sheet from the oven and allow

the cheese rounds to cool; they will crisp as they cool. Raise the oven temperature to 450°F.

3 Meanwhile, quarter the zucchini and yellow squash lengthwise. Cut each spear into 1-inch pieces on the bias, rotating the pieces after each cut so you end up with pieces that look like triangles with one rounded edge.

4 Toss the squash with the olive oil and salt on the other prepared baking sheet and spread out in a single layer. Roast, stirring occasionally, until the squash is tender and browned, about 35 minutes. Transfer to a serving dish.

5 Break the Parmesan crisps into small pieces and scatter them over the squash. Serve immediately.

WHY DIDN'T I THINK OF THAT?
MORE RECIPE IDEAS FROM LIDIA BASTIANICH

- Crumble a *frico* over risotto, a plate of pasta or vegetable soup.
- For a hot appetizer, sprinkle a base layer of cheese in a skillet over medium heat. Top it with sliced apples, slices of cooked potatoes or carrots or even sliced cooked sausage and broccoli rabe. Add another layer of grated cheese. As the bottom layers get crisp, the top layers of cheese will begin to melt. Use a spatula to flip the filled *fricos* and let them crisp on the other side. Top with microgreens.

chef tips from lidia bastianich

ON *FRICOS* You can drape the *frico* while it's still pliable over the handle of a wooden spoon suspended between two cans. It will cool in the shape of a taco shell and, when filled with a salad of lightly dressed baby greens, makes a spectacular first course. Made smaller—the size of a chocolate chip cookie—and draped over a spoon, *fricos* make a wonderful hors d'oeuvre on their own to have with cocktails.

ON THE BEST *FRICO* CHEESES Parmesan, Grana Padano and Montasio are great cheeses for *fricos*. Avoid soft, creamy cheeses because they won't get crisp. Avoid aged cheeses because their aroma will intensify and can become overpowering.

ON GRATING THE CHEESE FOR *FRICOS* The size of the cheese shavings is important. I like to grate the cheese to a medium coarseness to get crispy, lacy *fricos*. If the cheese is grated too fine, it will cook into a solid sheet and you stand a chance of burning it. If the grated cheese is too coarse, it will give a leathery texture to the *fricos*.

ON COOKING *FRICOS* Be sure to keep an eye on the cheese while it's cooking—if it burns even a little, it will become bitter. After you plate the *frico*, you can use a paper towel to blot up excess oil from the cheese.

Sweet Potato, Coconut + Five-Spice Gratin

" For Christmas one year, I elected to make a special meal, overruling a long-held family tradition of going out for Chinese food. The centerpiece was a standing rib roast, my single favorite cut of meat. Since that was quite conventional, I wanted to balance it with a more zingy side dish, which is how I landed on this Asian-spiced sweet potato gratin.

Though the potatoes can be easily sliced with a mandoline, I thought better of it. Chef David Chang has told me that he's seen lots of mandoline accidents in restaurant kitchens, so that seemed as good a reason as any not to use one on Christmas Day (that said, if you're fearless or accomplished, go right ahead). I sliced the sweet potatoes as evenly as I could, then poured the coconut milk with the five-spice powder over the potatoes and baked the gratin. It looked gorgeous when I presented it at the table, but it tasted as if someone had dumped the spice drawer into the gratin. (On a positive note, my mother, whose taste buds were dulled by a cold, thought it was terrific.) In order to avoid such a problem again, I asked for advice from chef Floyd Cardoz, whose food I loved at the Indian-fusion restaurant Tabla and also at North End Grill. His solution? Taste the coconut milk and spice mixture as you go and stop when it seems just right. I've adjusted the recipe here to have the proper amount of the pungent five-spice powder.

ACTIVE TIME: 20 MINUTES   TOTAL TIME: 1½ HOURS   SERVES 8

....

4 tablespoons (½ stick) unsalted butter, melted

One 13.5-ounce can full-fat coconut milk

½ cup heavy cream

¾ teaspoon five-spice powder

¼ teaspoon cayenne pepper

Kosher salt

2½ pounds sweet potatoes (about 4 medium), peeled

¾ cup panko bread crumbs

¾ cup unsweetened shredded coconut

1 Preheat the oven to 400°F. Brush a 3-quart (2-inch-deep) or 9-by-13-inch baking dish with half of the butter. Set aside.

2 Whisk together the coconut milk, heavy cream, five-spice powder, cayenne and 1½ teaspoons salt in a medium bowl.

3 Using a very sharp knife, thinly slice the sweet potatoes into rounds about ⅛ inch thick. Arrange half of the sliced sweet potatoes in the prepared baking dish in even layers. Pour half of the coconut milk mixture over the sweet potatoes. Repeat with the remaining potatoes and coconut milk mixture.

4 Cover the dish loosely with foil and bake the gratin until the sweet potatoes are nearly tender, about 45 minutes.

5 Meanwhile, in a small bowl, stir together the panko, coconut, the remaining butter and a pinch of salt to form coarse crumbs.

6 Remove the gratin from the oven and sprinkle the panko mixture evenly on top. Return it to the oven and bake until the top is golden brown, the sweet potatoes are completely cooked through and the liquid has been absorbed, 25 to 30 minutes. Let stand for 10 minutes, then serve.

WHY DIDN'T I THINK OF THAT?
ANOTHER RECIPE IDEA FROM FLOYD CARDOZ

- Try making the gratin with a paste instead of a spice blend: red curry paste, green curry paste, tandoori paste or vindaloo paste.

chef tips from **floyd cardoz**

ON SEASONING To avoid ruining an entire gratin by adding too much seasoning, add the five-spice powder to the coconut milk mixture a little at a time and taste as you go. If you add too much, the only way out is to make some more sauce with no spice and marry the two.

ON CHECKING FOR DONENESS Use a knife to check the consistency of the sweet potatoes while they're baking.

ON ENSURING EVEN COOKING If you've prepared your gratin in advance and chilled it, bring it to room temperature before you put it in the oven.

ON HOW TO IMPROVE DRY SWEET POTATOES The older the root vegetable, the less moisture it has. If you notice that your sweet potatoes are drier than normal when you slice them, let them sit in the coconut milk mixture for 30 minutes before baking. If they absorb most of the liquid, add a splash more.

ON FIXING A TOO-WET GRATIN In the event you don't have enough vegetables or add too much liquid (if it's sloshing around the dish or there is too much space between the vegetables), simply pour a bit out.

Broccoli Rabe Pizza

" Determined to make pizza, my family's favorite food and the zeitgeist dish of the millennium, I elected to start the easy way, with premade dough. So when I stopped off at Joanne Chang's Flour Bakery in Boston and saw gorgeous balls of dough wrapped in plastic, I bought one. During the long train ride to New York, it expanded, until it looked like a gargantuan heirloom tomato with deep ridges and creases.

When I got the dough home, I set to making the pizza right away, flattening it and trying to push it with my fingers into a big circle. The dough refused to stretch. Assuming that something happened to it on the ride, I gave up and just baked the rectangular lump of dough with broccoli rabe and a mix of cheeses and crème fraîche on top. Though it wasn't awful, it wasn't good either.

To improve my luck the next time around, I consulted with Nancy Silverton, who makes some of my favorite pizza in America at Mozza in LA, and I discovered that the dough most likely wasn't the problem after all. After the trip, it was rested and at room temperature, two important qualities for a pizza dough. I had given up too soon. Nancy told me I needed to work the dough into shape slowly, first tapping my fingers in the center of the dough, as if on piano keys, then draping the dough over my fists, moving them around like the hands of clock, to enlarge the shape.

ACTIVE TIME: 40 MINUTES   TOTAL TIME: 1 HOUR
MAKES ONE 10-BY-12-INCH PIZZA

¼ cup plus 2 tablespoons olive oil

1 garlic clove, minced

Pinch of crushed red pepper

1 small bunch broccoli rabe, trimmed and roughly chopped (about 3 cups)

Kosher salt

Flour for the work surface

1 pound store-bought pizza dough, at room temperature

3 to 4 tablespoons crème fraîche

1 cup coarsely shredded mozzarella cheese (don't use the fancy kind here)

½ cup finely grated Parmigiano-Reggiano cheese

Freshly ground black pepper

1 Position a rack in the lower third of the oven and preheat the oven to 450°F. Rub 2 tablespoons of the olive oil all over a large baking sheet.

2 Put 2 tablespoons of the olive oil in a large skillet set over medium-high heat, add the garlic and crushed red pepper and cook until fragrant, just a minute. Add the broccoli rabe and ½ cup water and season with salt. Cover the skillet and cook, uncovering to stir the broccoli rabe occasionally, until it's bright green and tender, about 6 minutes. Transfer the broccoli rabe to a plate and set aside to cool.

3 Dust your work surface with flour and place the dough on it. Since you're making a rectangular pizza, first form the dough into an oval. Starting in the center, tap the dough with your fingers, then move out to the edges to flatten it and go around the edges with two fingers. Flip the dough over and repeat. Drape the dough over your fists and move them around in a clockwise direction, letting gravity pull and stretch the dough, until it's about ¼ inch thick and about 10 by 12 inches. If the dough is being stubborn, simply return it to the work surface, cover it with a clean towel and let it rest for 10 minutes before trying again. You might have to do this a couple of times.

4 Transfer the dough to the prepared baking sheet. Using the back of a spoon, spread a very thin layer of crème fraîche over the dough. Scatter half of the mozzarella and half of the Parmesan on top. Scatter the broccoli rabe evenly on top of the cheese layer and then sprinkle with the remaining mozzarella and Parmesan. Drizzle the remaining 2 tablespoons of olive oil all over the pizza and sprinkle with pepper and a little bit of salt.

5 Bake the pizza until the bottom of the crust is golden brown and the topping is bubbly, about 12 to 15 minutes. Remove the pizza from the oven and let it cool for 5 minutes, then cut into squares and serve hot.

MAKE AHEAD The cooked broccoli rabe can be refrigerated for up to 3 days.

chef tips from **nancy silverton**

ON THE IMPORTANCE OF ROOM-TEMPERATURE DOUGH Don't ever try to shape dough that you've taken straight from the refrigerator—the warmer the dough, the more pliable it will be.

ON SHAPING THE PIZZA Flatten the rested dough with your hands and then go around the edges with two fingers to create a puffy center. Then flip the dough over and do the same to the other side. A silky dough basically stretches itself. And remember that pizza doesn't have to be round— it can still be delicious even if it's not!

ON EDITING YOUR PIZZA TOPPINGS The worst pizza is the one you order with "the works." You do not want to weigh down the dough with too many toppings. Edit your toppings.

ON PIZZA STONES A pizza stone or oven tile is helpful but not totally necessary. If you do have one, make sure it heats up for at least an hour in your oven. A good one is the metal pizza stone from Modernist Cuisine (modernistcuisine.com).

ON THE BEST OVEN For making pizza at home, a convection oven is best.

ON ENTERTAINING Set limits when you are first beginning—don't invite twenty people over, because they're all going to be standing around waiting for pizza. Make pizza for the family to start and limit the toppings.

ON PIZZA TOPPINGS

- Use bacon that is still raw—the bacon will cook completely in the oven. If you put cooked bacon on the pizza, it will burn.
- Sausage should be cooked slightly to render some of its fat before going on top of the pizza. If you put it on raw, the pizza will be greasy.
- Arugula is best added after the pizza is cooked.
- Escarole, a much sturdier green, can be put on a pizza raw and cooked in the oven.
- Mushrooms are far better if roasted first before going on top of your pizza.

My Favorite Vegetable Juice

66 From time to time, I order lunch at the office from a nearby takeout place that has earned the nickname Expensive Foods (the actual name is FreeFoods). Often I skip over the salads and go straight for one of the many vegetable juices—which led me to try making my own juice blend. Since my favorite combination at Expensive Foods is beet, ginger, celery, apple and cayenne, it was the first drink I tried at home. The juice was great, but I was not happy. The juicer had so many parts to wash! So much pulp just went into the garbage! Then I experimented with blitzing vegetables in my blender, and I found I could get a great consistency without all that onerous cleanup. A high-powered blender, such as a Vitamix, is crazy expensive, but since juices sold at a shop can cost $8 each, I figure it more than pays for itself in the long run.

TOTAL TIME: 10 MINUTES   SERVES 1

1 large beet, scrubbed and cut into chunks
One 1-inch piece of ginger, roughly chopped
2 celery stalks
1 apple, roughly chopped
¼ teaspoon cayenne pepper

Feed the beets, ginger, celery and apple into your juicer, collecting the juice in a large glass. Whisk in the cayenne pepper. (Alternatively, you can put all of the fruit and vegetables in a powerful blender, along with the cayenne and ¼ cup water, blend them together and pass the mixture through a fine-mesh strainer into a glass.) Drink immediately.

braised chicken with leeks, mushrooms + peas, page 102

poultry

Braised Chicken with Leeks, Mushrooms + Peas

66 When I'm cooking at home, I'm usually the only one in the kitchen, which means I'm usually the only one intimately aware of my mistakes. This is both good (it's less embarrassing) and bad (it means I don't have a teacher helping me on my journey as a cook). But the day I made a chicken in Riesling inspired by a recipe from Jean-Georges Vongerichten, *Top Chef* winner Kristen Kish was at my side cheering me along, coaching me as I faltered. (She was also chopping and sautéing butternut squash, yellow squash and eggplant for a pasta sauce and teaching my kids how to roll sheets of dough through the pasta machine. The ability of chefs to multitask always astonishes me.) I was taking the chicken out of the pan when she scooted over and put the offending too-pale pieces back on the heat. She not only got a lot more color on the skin, but she seared the edges to be sure they were browned too. With her right there, I finally understood how brown the chicken needed to be—as well as the problem with shortcuts. As I all but begged to move the meal along, she insisted we take the necessary time to caramelize the skin: she wanted to render the fat to avoid a greasy sauce and to add flavor. Kristen's patience in cooking was a reminder that in the kitchen, as in life, to get the best results, you need to do the work—and do it right.

ACTIVE TIME: 1 HOUR   TOTAL TIME: 1½ HOURS   SERVES 4

¼ cup grapeseed oil, divided

3½ pounds bone-in chicken parts (wings, thighs, legs and/or halved breasts), trimmed of excess skin and patted dry with paper towels

Kosher salt and freshly ground black pepper

2 large leeks, white and light green parts only, thinly sliced and thoroughly washed (about 1 heaping cup)

1 cup Riesling

½ cup chicken stock or low-sodium chicken broth

3 tablespoons unsalted butter

½ pound cremini mushrooms, cleaned and quartered

⅓ cup heavy cream

2 cups frozen peas

1 Heat 2 tablespoons of the oil in a very large enameled cast-iron casserole over medium-high heat until shimmering. Season half of the chicken liberally with salt and pepper and add it to the casserole. Cook, turning the chicken pieces occasionally, until well browned all over, 15 to 20 minutes; turn the heat down to medium if the brown bits in the pan are getting too dark. Transfer the browned chicken to a plate. Season the remaining chicken with salt and pepper and repeat the browning with the remaining 2 tablespoons of oil. Transfer the second batch of chicken to the plate and set aside.

2 Discard all but a very thin layer of fat from the casserole. Add the leeks to the pot and cook, stirring, until softened, about 4 minutes. Add the Riesling and chicken stock, turn the heat to high and bring to a boil, scraping up the browned bits from the bottom of the casserole.

3 Turn the heat down to low and return all of the chicken to the pot, along with any juices that have accumulated on the plate. Cover the casserole and gently simmer the chicken until it's cooked through, about 20 minutes.

4 Meanwhile, melt the butter in a large skillet over medium-high heat and let cook until it just starts to turn brown, 1 to 2 minutes. Add the mushrooms, season with a large pinch of salt and a few grinds of pepper and cook, stirring occasionally, until the mushrooms are softened and browned all over, about 10 minutes.

5 Transfer the mushrooms to the casserole with the chicken. Add the cream and peas, stir everything together and cook just until the peas are hot and bright green, about 3 minutes. Season with salt and pepper and serve immediately.

SERVE WITH Rice or egg noodles.
MAKE AHEAD The braised chicken (before adding the mushrooms and peas) can be refrigerated for up to 3 days. Reheat over medium-low heat before proceeding.

chef tips from
kristen kish

ON COOKING OIL Grapeseed oil has a much higher smoking point than olive oil and is virtually flavorless. It will allow you to get the pot hot enough to render out the fat from the chicken and to brown the skin without burning it.

ON COLOR Look for a beautiful even brown: think of a perfectly toasted hazelnut.

ON CHECKING FOR DONENESS It takes practice to tell when chicken is cooked through. Anything is better than stabbing it. Use your fingers; it should feel firm to the touch. An instant-read thermometer also works great; just make sure it's accurate. Another option is a cake tester (that stainless steel pick with a blue tab)—insert it into the thigh and then touch it; if it's hot, the chicken is cooked all the way through.

Four-Chile Chicken

" The first time I made this Yucatán chicken dish, inspired by one from Latin chef Jose Garces of Amada in Philadelphia, just finding the right chiles was stressful. The recipe I started with called for a whole dried guajillo chile, ground chipotle chile powder and a fresh habañero pepper, which were all in different aisles. Then I discovered that the chiles on the shelves didn't match the ones in the recipe. Without knowing a lot about chiles, I had no real idea how to make substitutions. I bought one of each of the available chiles—powdered, dried and fresh. When I got home, I did some quick research and realized the chile family was too complicated to understand if I wanted to get dinner on the table before midnight. So I powered on, making substitutions willy-nilly. The chicken was mildly spicy with a great taste of pineapple, but I was still troubled by my free fall through the world of chiles. I reached out to Jose, who recommended substituting chiles with similar flavor profiles. So, for a hot, smoky dried chile powder like chipotle, swap in cayenne and smoked paprika. For a fruity dried chile like guajillo, trade in ancho chile. I may miss the nuances of more unusual chiles, but with these very general guidelines in mind, I can still make a dish that tastes great. Here I've steamlined the original dish, and hopefully minimized the chile challenges.

ACTIVE TIME: 1½ HOURS   TOTAL TIME: 3 HOURS   SERVES 6 TO 8

FOR THE SPICE RUB

¼ cup olive oil

2 tablespoons sugar

1 tablespoon kosher salt

1 tablespoon sweet smoked paprika

1½ teaspoons cayenne pepper

2 teaspoons ground allspice

2 teaspoons freshly ground black pepper

2 teaspoons ground cumin

1 teaspoon ground cinnamon

Pinch of ground cloves

7 to 8 pounds bone-in chicken parts (wings, thighs, legs and/
   or halved breasts; 16 to 20 pieces), trimmed of excess skin and
   patted dry with paper towels

FOR THE SAUCE

2 guajillo or ancho chiles (see Notes), stemmed, seeded and broken into large pieces

½ cup water

Finely grated zest of 2 oranges (about 1½ tablespoons)

1½ cups freshly squeezed orange juice

1½ cups apple cider vinegar

¾ cup honey

2 cups diced fresh pineapple

½ cup chopped peeled ginger

1 canned chipotle chile in adobo sauce, plus 1 tablespoon of the sauce

2 jalapeños, stemmed, seeded and coarsely chopped

Kosher salt

1 For the rub, mix the olive oil, sugar, salt and spices in a small bowl.

2 Put the chicken in a large baking dish. Pour the rub over the chicken and rub it into each piece. Cover the chicken and marinate at room temperature for 30 minutes, or in the refrigerator for up to 24 hours. If it's been refrigerated, bring the chicken to room temperature, about 30 minutes, before cooking.

3 Meanwhile, make the sauce: Put the guajillos and water in a small saucepan, turn the heat to high and bring to a boil, then turn off the heat. Let the guajillos stand until softened, about 15 minutes.

4 Add the orange zest and juice, vinegar, honey, pineapple, ginger, chipotle, adobo sauce and jalapeño to the saucepan and bring the mixture to a boil. Cook until the liquid is reduced by half, about 20 minutes. Let cool to warm.

5 Transfer the chile mixture to a blender and puree until smooth. Alternatively, use an immersion blender. Scrape the puree back into the saucepan and simmer over medium heat until reduced to about 2 cups, about 7 minutes. Season to taste with salt and set aside.

6 To finish the dish, preheat the oven to 400°F.

7 Transfer the chicken pieces to two foil-lined rimmed baking sheets, leaving a little space around the pieces. Roast the chicken until it's just cooked through (an instant-read thermometer inserted in a thigh near the bone should reach 165°F), about 30 minutes.

8 Remove the chicken from the oven and turn on the broiler. Working with one sheet of chicken at a time, brush some sauce over the chicken pieces. Broil until the sauce is bubbling and glazed, about 2 minutes or so, depending on the strength of your broiler. Be sure to check frequently so that it doesn't burn. Carefully flip the pieces, brush with more sauce and broil the other side.

9 Serve the chicken immediately, with the remaining sauce.

NOTES A guajillo is a dried mirasol chile and an ancho is a dried poblano pepper. A chipotle is a smoke-dried jalapeño.

MAKE AHEAD The spice rub, without the oil, can be stored in a covered container at room temperature for up to 2 months. The sauce can be stored in a covered container in the refrigerator for up to a week.

chef tips from **jose garces**

ON CHOOSING CHILE POWDER Chipotle chile powder can be replaced by any good standard chile powder. If you can, sniff out one that's slightly smoky, since that's the flavor profile of chipotles.

ON MAKING CHILES LESS SPICY To cut down on their heat factor, remove the seeds from canned chipotles in adobo sauce or fresh chiles like jalapeños.

ON THE IMPORTANCE OF GEOGRAPHY Group chiles geographically and use accordingly. For Mexican cuisine, stick to guajillos, anchos, mulatos, chipotles, jalapeños and poblanos. For Caribbean cuisine, use Fresnos, cachuchas and Scotch bonnets. For Peruvian and Ecuadorian food, use ají amarillo, ají panca and ají rocoto chiles.

ON BOOSTING THE FLAVOR OF DRIED CHILES Toasting dried chiles will heighten their flavors by bringing out their essential oils. You must be very careful not to overtoast them, though, or they will become bitter.

ON HANDLING CHILES If you're working with spicy chiles, wear latex gloves so you don't burn your skin.

CHEF VARIATION Use ground chiles as a garnish on top of a finished dish to add an extra splash of spice and visual interest.

Chili of Forgiveness

66 Chili is the beginning cook's dream. The recipe is very forgiving, and even if you make a small mistake or two, you can still arrive at a delicious dish. I learned just how true this is when I set out to make a big batch of a Mediterranean-inspired chili. I couldn't find ground dark-meat turkey at the market, so I bought ground turkey breast. But when I took it out of the packaging, it was revoltingly mushy and I threw it out. Luckily, I had ground pork in my fridge (you can use either turkey or pork here). The recipe called for canned diced tomatoes, but I only had cans of whole tomatoes, so I used them. I hate peeling squash, so I'd bought peeled, cut butternut squash. Unfortunately, it was dried out, so instead of cooking in twenty minutes, it took upward of an hour.

After the squash was finally tender, I reached into the pantry for a can of white beans. What I found looked like mini versions of the cannellini beans the recipe called for. What the heck, I'd switched everything else, so I tossed them in with bravado. I served the chili to a group of friends, who all asked for seconds. But it taught me a big lesson: I should have planned better. If you're prepared, you never have to depend on luck—or a forgiving recipe—to get you through.

ACTIVE TIME: 30 MINUTES   TOTAL TIME: 1½ HOURS   SERVES 8

¼ cup olive oil

1 large red onion, finely diced (about 1½ cups)

6 garlic cloves, minced

2 tablespoons finely chopped rosemary

Kosher salt

2 teaspoons crushed red pepper

1½ pounds ground dark-meat turkey (you can substitute lean ground pork)

Two 28-ounce cans whole peeled tomatoes, drained, juices reserved, and chopped

4 cups diced butternut squash (see Note)

Two 15-ounce cans cannellini beans, drained and rinsed

1 pound Tuscan kale (also called dinosaur or Lacinato kale), stems discarded, leaves roughly chopped (about 8 cups)

12 large sage leaves, finely sliced

Freshly grated Parmesan cheese, for serving

1 Put the olive oil in a large heavy pot set over medium-high heat, add the onion, garlic, rosemary and a large pinch of salt and cook, stirring occasionally, until the onion is just barely softened, about 5 minutes. Add the crushed red pepper and toast for 30 seconds.

2 Add the turkey and cook, stirring occasionally, until the meat is cooked through and quite browned and its moisture has evaporated, 10 to 15 minutes.

3 Add the tomatoes and their juices to the pot, along with another big pinch of salt, increase the heat to high and bring the mixture to a boil. Turn the heat to low and gently simmer, uncovered, until the tomatoes lose their tin-can taste, about 20 minutes.

4 Stir in the squash, cover the pot and cook over medium-low heat, stirring occasionally, until the squash is just tender, about 20 minutes.

5 Add the beans, kale and sage and cook, uncovered, until the kale is just wilted, about 5 minutes. Season with salt.

6 Ladle the chili into bowls and top each portion with grated Parmesan.

NOTE A small-to-medium butternut squash (about 1½ pounds) will yield 4 cups of diced (¾-inch) squash. You can also find it already peeled and cubed in many produce sections, but make sure it's fresh looking, not dried out. You can also substitute sweet potatoes, which are easier to peel and cut. The chili will be sweeter but still delicious.

MAKE AHEAD The chili can be refrigerated for up to 1 week. Reheat it over medium-low heat, stirring often. It also freezes very well for up to 2 months.

Greek Chicken Salad

66 My husband, Barclay, is the leftovers king. He is always happy to take a Tupperware container of last night's dinner to work for lunch. He's as delighted to discover the kids' uneaten vegetables as he is to find the remains of a meal from one of New York City's finest restaurants. But there is one exception, and that's chicken. He doesn't like chicken, broiled, roasted, fried or sautéed, for dinner and he certainly won't eat it as leftovers. I love all kinds of chicken, but I'm not a fan of leftovers, including chicken leftovers. To solve the family food riddle—how can I indulge in my love of chicken and still provide Barclay with a good lunch?—I experimented like mad with cold chicken. He was stalwart in his refusal of chicken redux: he'd turned down chicken soup, chicken tacos, chicken sandwiches. But then, rather unexpectedly, he enthusiastically endorsed this chicken salad, with its creamy feta and yogurt dressing, the briny olives, crisp cucumbers and pita chips.

TOTAL TIME: 20 MINUTES   SERVES 4 FOR LUNCH

1 cup (about 4 ounces) crumbled feta cheese
1 cup plain whole-milk Greek yogurt
¼ cup freshly squeezed lemon juice
2 teaspoons dried oregano
½ teaspoon kosher salt
1 teaspoon freshly ground black pepper
4 cups diced cooked chicken (preferably a mix of white and dark meat)
1 large cucumber, halved lengthwise, seeded and cut into ½-inch dice
1 small red onion, finely diced
1 cup Kalamata olives, pitted and roughly chopped
3 cups plain pita chips, lightly crushed

1 Put the feta, yogurt, lemon juice, oregano, salt and pepper in a blender and puree until smooth.
2 Combine the chicken with the cucumber, onion, olives and pita chips in a large bowl. Toss with the dressing and serve.

Chicken Thighs with Smoky Vietnamese Caramel Sauce

❝ My friend Suzie, whose family came to the United States as refugees from Vietnam, inspired me to make this dish. She insisted that it was easy, something her relatives back home would make often. Her confidence helped me overcome my fear of making anything with caramel (in the past, I'd always ruined it). Suzie also gave me a good tip: her family made the sauce with a little brewed Lapsang souchong tea. I didn't ruin the caramel this time, but once I had a nice dark caramel, I added the chile, red onion, ginger, pepper and tea and the whole thing seized. Initially I was patient, because Suzie's instructions had warned me that the caramel might harden and then relax, and it did liquefy—but not completely. A dark lump of caramel remained, looking like a toad lurking below the brown surface. I could finish the sauce, but I was frustrated! How was I supposed to dissolve the lump?

Andrew Zimmern of Bizarre Foods fame, who's eaten and cooked all over the world, had the answer straightaway: the pesky lump of caramel would have taken care of itself if I'd waited longer. Panic and frustration are enemies of excellence in the kitchen.

TOTAL TIME: 45 MINUTES   SERVES 4 TO 6

....

2 Lapsang souchong tea bags

¾ cup boiling water

1 cup sugar

1 teaspoon freshly squeezed lemon juice

1 small red chile, split down the middle

3 tablespoons finely diced red onion or shallot

One 2-inch piece of ginger, peeled and minced

2 teaspoons very coarsely ground black pepper, or more to taste

3 tablespoons fish sauce, or more to taste

2 tablespoons canola oil

12 skinless bone-in chicken thighs (about 3¾ pounds), patted dry
    with paper towels

Kosher salt

1 Put the tea bags in a mug and cover with the boiling water. Set aside while you make the caramel.

2 Put the sugar and lemon juice in a small heavy saucepan and cook over low heat, without stirring, until the sugar dissolves, about 5 minutes. Holding the saucepan by the handle, gently swirl the pan as the sugar slowly caramelizes. Small bubbles will form around the edges and grow larger and move toward the center of the pan and the mixture will come to a vigorous boil. Let it cook until it becomes the color of dark tea, about 5 minutes longer. Then remove the pan from the heat and gently swirl it again, watching the color deepen even further. You want it to become the color of molasses. The whole process will take about 20 minutes. Whatever you do, don't stir!

3 Carefully add the chile, red onion, ginger and pepper; the hot caramel will bubble up. Pour the reserved tea into the caramel, discarding the tea bags (the caramel may initially seize, but don't worry—it will eventually dissolve). Cook the sauce over low heat until the caramel dissolves and the sauce is thickened, about 5 minutes. Stir in the fish sauce, then season the sauce to taste with more fish sauce and/or black pepper if necessary. Set the sauce aside.

4 Heat the canola oil in a large Dutch oven over medium-high heat until shimmering. Gently place the chicken thighs in the pot in a single layer, working in batches if necessary to avoid crowding. Cook the chicken, seasoning the pieces with salt and turning them occasionally, until beautifully browned all over, about 10 minutes.

5 Carefully pour the caramel sauce over the chicken, turn the heat to low and simmer, turning the thighs occasionally, until the chicken is tender and the sauce has become a shiny, thick glaze, about 10 minutes. Discard the chile.

6 Transfer the chicken to a platter and drizzle over the remaining sauce.

SERVE WITH Steamed bok choy.

NOTES The tea adds a nice smokiness, but water can be used in a pinch. You want a dark caramel for this sauce, but caramel can go from dark to burnt very quickly, and the latter tastes awfully bitter. Keep a close eye on the caramel during the last stage of cooking, before adding the hot tea.

MAKE AHEAD The entire dish can be refrigerated for up to 3 days. Reheat over medium-low heat. Alternatively, the sauce can be refrigerated for up to 1 week.

chef tips from **andrew zimmern**

ON THE PERFECT PAN SIZE
With caramel, don't work
too big—if the pan is too
wide, there's too much
space in which caramel can
burn.

**ON AVOIDING
CRYSTALLIZING SUGAR** A
few drops of lemon juice will
help the sugar melt more
evenly.

**ON SWIRLING, NOT
STIRRING, CARAMEL**
Once the sugar is about
60 percent melted, start
to swirl the pan for even
cooking, being careful to
avoid getting any caramel
on the sides. Don't stir, just
tilt and swirl. Everyone's
inclination is to get in there
and stir and blast it with
heat, but that will cause
the caramel to carbonize
and create steam, which
will rise and then fall back
in and make it bitter. This
is the one exception to the
rule that I always tell home
cooks, which is to "Cook
hotter."

ON SEIZING CARAMEL If
the caramel seizes, don't
worry—let it take care of
itself. As long as you're
patient, it will cooperate.

ON TESTING CARAMEL To
test caramel sauce, put a
spoonful of the sauce on a
clean plate and let it cool
to room temperature. This
will indicate how viscous the
sauce is, and it will also cool
it quickly so you can taste
it without burning your
tongue.

**ON THE FLAVOR OF
CARAMEL** Keep in mind that
you want the flavor very
strong here—it's a sauce,
not a soup, and it will be
tempered by the other
ingredients.

**ON MAKING THE SAUCE
AHEAD** The sauce won't
go bad: you're essentially
combining ingredients
that preserve—sugar and
fish sauce. In Vietnam,
this is one of the "mother
sauces." Instead of a pantry
with spices, there are jars
and bottles of caramel
sauce, chile paste, etc. At
a Chinese restaurant, you
don't see the speed rack
of spices you'd see in a
Western kitchen—instead,
there are squeeze bottles
of the sauces. If you were a
Vietnamese grandmother,
you'd make this sauce once
a month, or even every
couple of months.

Fried Chicken

> Fried chicken is my favorite food, hands down. I've conducted my own fried-chicken city tours from New York to Nashville and I am devoted to the all-American style, with a crispy thin coating and juicy meat. Until recently, I had been too scared of cooking in bubbling oil to try it. As someone who can ruin quinoa, frying chicken seems downright dangerous. But since part of the challenge in becoming a better cook is overcoming my fear of failure, I finally mustered the courage to do so. I gently placed the first pieces of marinated chicken in the hot oil. It bubbled, but not too much. I turned the pieces, but not too often, and I pulled them out after about 15 minutes, when the skin had darkened. I couldn't wait—I had to try it right away. It was great! Feeling confident, I started on round two. This time the oil was going crazy, boiling up around the pieces. This struck me as a good thing, since the oil for frying is supposed to be hot, hot, hot, but when I pulled out the legs and thighs, they were too brown, almost burnt, and the meat wasn't fully cooked.

The next day, in the *Food & Wine* test kitchen, I began to tell the team my story, that my chicken had burned and . . . They cut me off. "Did you forget to turn down the heat so the oil didn't get too hot?" Technically, I didn't forget, because I didn't know I was supposed to do that. But now I do. And so do you. I asked fried chicken expert Marcus Samuelsson of Red Rooster in Harlem to give me more pointers; see his Chef Tips on page 121.

ACTIVE TIME: 1 HOUR   TOTAL TIME: 1 HOUR + AT LEAST 4 HOURS MARINATING   SERVES 8

2 cups buttermilk

3 tablespoons kosher salt, divided

3 tablespoons freshly ground black pepper, divided

1 tablespoon cayenne pepper

1 tablespoon paprika

Two 3-pound chickens, cut into 10 pieces each (2 wings, 2 legs, 2 thighs and each breast cut in half across the bone), or 5 pounds bone-in chicken parts, trimmed of excess skin and patted dry with paper towels

2 cups all-purpose flour

¼ cup cornstarch

Peanut oil, for frying

1 Whisk together the buttermilk, 2 tablespoons of the salt, 2 tablespoons of the black pepper, the cayenne and the paprika in a small bowl. Put the chicken in two gallon-sized resealable plastic bags. Divide the marinade between them, seal the bags and turn to coat the chicken thoroughly. Refrigerate for at least 4 hours, and up to 24 hours.

2 Remove the chicken from the refrigerator an hour before you're ready to cook.

3 Preheat the oven to 250°F. Set two cooling racks on two rimmed baking sheets. Put one of them in the oven and set the other one near the stove. Have an instant-read thermometer ready.

4 Combine the flour and cornstarch in a large baking dish and whisk in the remaining 1 tablespoon each salt and black pepper.

5 Pour ½ inch of oil into a large cast-iron or other heavy skillet, and heat over medium heat until the oil reaches 350°F.

6 Meanwhile, take a few pieces of chicken out of one bag, allowing the excess buttermilk to drip back in, and dredge the chicken lightly on all sides in the flour mixture, tapping off the excess coating. You are looking for a very light coating with no wet spots.

7 Gently place the dredged chicken into the hot oil–don't crowd the pieces—and fry over medium heat; the goal is to keep the oil temperature between 300° and 325°F. Cook the chicken, turning every few minutes, until the skin is dark golden brown. It will take about 7 minutes for the wings and smaller breast pieces, 10 to 15 minutes for the drumsticks and large breast pieces and 15 to 20 minutes for the thighs; the internal temperature should reach 160°F. As each piece is done, transfer it to the baking sheet near the stove to drain, then transfer it to the baking sheet in the oven to keep warm and crisp.

8 Dredge and fry the remaining chicken in batches. Add more oil to the skillet if necessary and heat it well before frying. Serve the chicken hot.

NOTES Heat the frying oil to a higher temperature to start, because adding the chicken will bring the temperature down. Check the temperature of the chicken when it's out of the pot, not in the oil—poking the chicken releases juices, which will cause the oil to sputter. As you cook, you will notice where the hot spots are in the skillet—so be sure to move thinner pieces away from the hot spots, or they will cook too quickly.

WHY DIDN'T I THINK OF THAT?
MORE RECIPE IDEAS FROM MARCUS SAMUELSSON

- For extra-crunchy chicken, add finely chopped water chestnuts to the dredging flour.
- For the crispiest chicken, fry it twice: The first time you fry it, the heat of the oil should be lower to get the bird tender on the inside, like a French fry. Cook it through at this temperature (it's essentially the same thing as poaching). The second time the oil should be at a higher temperature, to make the chicken crunchy on the outside. It will fry very quickly the second time.

chef tips from
marcus samuelsson

ON THE OPTIMAL CHICKEN SIZE The most important thing when making fried chicken is to choose a bird that's not too big, as it's likely to be watery. Stick to a 3-pound chicken and make sure it's firm.

ON BONELESS CHICKEN Don't fry boneless chicken—you'll lose moisture and flavor.

ON THE BEST OIL FOR FRYING Use peanut oil for frying. (If a guest is allergic, substitute canola oil.)

ON KEEPING FRIED CHICKEN CRISP Never cover fried chicken with foil after cooking it. It will steam, and nobody wants soggy fried chicken.

Roast Chicken with Garam Masala–Ginger Butter

66 Burnished skin. In two words, that's what I want from roast chicken. Is that so much to ask? Yes, I also want it to be juicy and tasty, but seriously, flabby skin is not appetizing. (One of my roast chickens looked like an oversized albino frog with wings.) I'd tried many methods and failed with all of them: starting with high heat, then lowering the temperature; salting the skin; massaging the skin with oil; putting butter under the skin but not on it. There were probably a dozen more techniques I could have tried, but I wasn't convinced I'd succeed with any of them either. So I asked legendary chef Thomas Keller of The French Laundry to show me his foolproof method, which relies on three important steps to achieve the perfect roast chicken: Air-dry the bird to pull the moisture out of the skin for at least 2 hours or as much as 2 days. Make sure the bird is at room temperature before you put it in the oven. And for us home cooks, don't truss it, so that air can circulate around the legs.

ACTIVE TIME: 10 MINUTES   TOTAL TIME: 1½ HOURS + AT LEAST
3 HOURS AIR-DRYING BEFORE ROASTING   SERVES 4

4 tablespoons (½ stick) unsalted butter, at room temperature
2 teaspoons kosher salt
2 teaspoons garam masala
2 teaspoons finely grated peeled ginger
One 3½- to 4-pound chicken—patted dry with paper towels and
    allowed to sit, uncovered, in the refrigerator for 2 to 3 hours, then
    preferably at room temperature for about 1 hour

1 Preheat the oven to 400°F.

2 In a small bowl, use a fork to mash the butter together with the salt, garam masala and ginger.

3 Use your fingers to carefully loosen the skin over the chicken breast and thighs. Spread one-third of the butter between the meat and skin, then rub the remaining butter over the entire surface of the chicken. Put the chicken in an ovenproof skillet or roasting pan and transfer it to the oven. Roast until the chicken is browned and an instant-read thermometer inserted into the thickest part of the thigh registers 165°F, about 50 minutes. Remove the chicken from the oven, transfer it to a cutting board and let it rest for at least 15 minutes before carving and serving.

chef tips from **thomas keller**

ON TRUSSING Professional chefs love to truss chickens—the breast cooks beautifully this way, but the legs are a bit underdone. At the restaurant, we're not serving the breast and legs at the same time, so we have the luxury of finishing the legs separately. For ease of cooking, however, I recommend that home cooks don't truss when roasting a whole chicken—the legs and thighs are denser than the breast and therefore take longer to cook. When you leave the legs untrussed, air will circulate around them and the chicken will cook more evenly.

ON PANS Don't worry too much about your roasting pan. When you're cooking in the oven, the heat is coming mainly from the environment, not from the vessel you're roasting in. You can roast a turkey in a throwaway aluminum foil pan and it will turn out just fine!

ON ALTERNATIVES TO AIR-DRYING If you don't have time to air-dry the chicken, start it at 450°F and roast for 10 to 15 minutes, then dial the temperature down to 375°F. If you can't get evaporation through air-drying, blasting initially with heat will help.

ON EVEN COOKING Don't keep checking on the chicken as it roasts. Opening the oven door repeatedly will bring the temperature down and the chicken won't cook as evenly.

ON READING CHICKEN JUICES Read the juices—if they're clear, the chicken will be overcooked because it will continue to cook once you take it out of the oven. It's all about time and temperature.

ON LETTING CHICKEN REST Let the chicken rest for at least 15 minutes or up to half an hour before carving it. It will continue to cook (through "carry-over cooking") after you remove it from the oven and the temperature will even out throughout the bird. Letting the chicken rest also creates anticipation—the aromas are there and everyone wants to know, _"When are we going to eat?"_

ON THE PLEASURES OF ROAST CHICKEN Remember that a roast chicken has a certain amount of forgiveness built in. As long as it's not drastically overcooked, everyone's still going to be satisfied. All the different areas give you different pleasures (the wing tips, the oysters, picking the carcass, etc.), so the entire experience forgives a bird that is slightly overcooked in some places.

Chicken Stir-Fry with Celery + Peanuts

66 Until recently, whenever I made stir-fried chicken with vegetables, I was disappointed. It was really bland, as if all I was doing was sautéing except on a higher heat, with a splash of soy sauce at the end. Then everything changed when *Bizarre Food* host Andrew Zimmern shared his recipe and technique. It involved more work, but the result was infinitely more nuanced and delicious. First he showed me how to flip ingredients in a pan without a spatula, using peanuts until I got the hang of it. He taught me to thrust the pan quickly forward and then pull back, which is incredibly awkward at first. After a few practice rounds, I got to use raw chicken chunks, which I tossed in the air and then saw land on the floor. I did learn something important as I picked up the pieces. Andrew asked me what it felt like. "It's slippery," I said. "Exactly. That's the feel of velveted chicken. It gets that way from the cornstarch." The next time, the chicken stayed in the pan and I tossed in snow peas and water chestnuts. As the stir-fry cooked, the drippings got crusty and brown—what I would have called a fail, until Andrew instructed me to pour in a bit of water. All of a sudden, the browned bits released from the pan and made the most astonishing sauce. And when I mixed in the fragrant sautéed ginger, shallot, scallion, garlic, celery, peanuts and sugar, I knew I had a new favorite weeknight dish.

TOTAL TIME: 30 MINUTES   SERVES 4

1½ pounds boneless, skinless chicken thighs, cut into 1-inch pieces

1 tablespoon sambal oelek (Asian chile sauce)

1 tablespoon cornstarch

1 tablespoon rice wine or sake (or rice vinegar)

¼ cup soy sauce, divided

¼ cup vegetable or peanut oil

One 2-inch piece of ginger, peeled and cut into thin matchsticks

2 garlic cloves, minced

2 scallions, thinly sliced, white and green parts kept separate

2 small celery stalks, thinly sliced, plus ½ cup roughly chopped celery leaves

2 large shallots, halved lengthwise and thinly sliced

2 teaspoons sugar

¼ cup unsalted dry-roasted peanuts

½ pound snow peas, ends trimmed
¼ cup drained and sliced water chestnuts
Kosher salt
1 hot red chile, thinly sliced (optional)

1 Put the chicken in a large bowl. Add the sambal oelek, cornstarch, rice wine and 2 tablespoons of the soy sauce and toss to coat. Set aside.

2 Set a large heavy skillet over very high heat and add 2 tablespoons of the oil. When the oil ripples (Andrew refers to this as "when it smiles"), add the ginger, garlic and scallion greens and cook over high heat, stirring, until fragrant, about 30 seconds. Add the celery, celery leaves, shallots, sugar and peanuts and cook, stirring, until the vegetables are crisp-tender, about 2 minutes. Transfer the mixture to a plate and set aside.

3 Add the remaining 2 tablespoons of oil to the skillet and let it get quite hot over medium-high heat. Add the chicken in a single layer and let it sit for a moment before stirring, then cook, stirring, until well browned and nearly cooked through, about 5 minutes. Add the snow peas and water chestnuts and cook, stirring, until the snow peas are bright green and crisp-tender, about 3 minutes.

4 Add the reserved ginger and celery mixture, along with the final 2 tablespoons of soy sauce and a couple tablespoons of water, and scrape up the flavorful bits stuck to the bottom of the pan with a wooden spoon. Then stir everything together and season to taste with salt.

5 Transfer the chicken to a platter and scatter the scallion whites and chile, if using, on top. Serve immediately.

chef tips from **andrew zimmern**

ON CUTTING CHICKEN Cut boneless chicken thighs into 3 sections. Then cut each third into an even dice.

ON CORNSTARCH Don't be afraid to use cornstarch. It helps tighten the sauce and gives the chicken a twice-cooked slippery quality that people associate with good Chinese wok cookery. It makes the meat soft and tender.

ON THE SMARTEST ADDITION TO A STIR-FRY Celery has a very strong flavor (think about its effect in chicken stock) that makes it a staple of Chinese cooking.

ON PREPPING GINGER Use a spoon to scrape off the skin. Then cut a thin slice off one side so it sits flat on the cutting board and you're not fighting a ball as you slice it.

ON SOY SAUCE Be sure to taste your soy sauce before using it. Soy sauce that's been sitting in your cupboard or refrigerator will be stronger because some of the liquid will have evaporated.

ON SCALLIONS Use scallions in cooking and for finishing a dish too. The green parts have a tart acidity—a nice balance to the sweetness of the cooked whites.

ON FLIPPING INGREDIENTS IN A PAN To learn to flip ingredients as you sauté, practice with peanuts or dried beans (something easy to pick up and cheap!). You're just pushing them up and then catching them. Push and catch, push and catch. But don't throw them up too high.

CHEF VARIATION To "velvet" the chicken, soak it overnight in a mixture of cornstarch, rice wine and chiles and then stir-fry it.

Simplest Roast Turkey

❝ Thanksgiving should be my big holiday, the highlight of my year of entertaining. But it isn't. My mother gathers the family every year and wouldn't hear of anyone else hosting. As a result, I never cook the Thanksgiving meal. So I decided I'd throw a TGIF party the day after Thanksgiving and make a turkey. I thought I was off to a great start. I received a magnificent free-range KellyBronze turkey. It arrived in a box with very specific cooking instructions, including "Start with the bird breast side down." The skin was silky, gorgeous with a few black bits of feathers sticking out. It felt very special, this bird. I looked at it lovingly and then put the domed part of the bird facedown and slid the pan into the oven. Halfway through roasting, I removed the pan from the oven to flip the turkey over. I stuck a wooden spoon into each end of the bird and attempted to lift this hot 15-pound beast. As I did, the turkey slid in circles over the spoons, and to my horror, a large swath of skin that had stuck to the bottom of the pan tore clean away from the breast! Not only did I scald myself with steam coming from the turkey cavity, I had a turkey with a large, ugly bald spot. Later, I explained what happened to Jonathan Waxman of Barbuto in New York City, who set my mind at ease. He is the Zen master of birds. Jonathan always roasts breast side up and never turns it over. And if the breast is darkening too quickly, he suggests just covering it with foil. Thank you, Mr. Stress-free Thanksgiving!

ACTIVE TIME: 15 MINUTES   TOTAL TIME: 3½ HOURS, LARGELY UNATTENDED + AT LEAST 8 HOURS DRY-BRINING + 45 MINUTES RESTING   SERVES 10, WITH LEFTOVERS

....

One 13- to 15-pound fresh turkey, patted dry with paper towels
2 tablespoons kosher salt
1½ teaspoons freshly ground black pepper
¼ cup olive oil

1 Early in the day, or the night before cooking, season the cavity and outside of the turkey with the salt and pepper. Place the bird breast side up on a rack in a roasting pan and let it sit, uncovered, in the refrigerator for at least 8 hours, or overnight.

2 Pull out your turkey and let it come to room temperature for 1 hour before cooking it.

3 Position a rack in the center of the oven and preheat the oven to 425°F.

4 Rub the olive oil all over the turkey. Roast the turkey for 1 hour, or until light golden.

5 Reduce the oven temperature to 375°F and roast for 2 to 2¼ hours longer, until richly browned and an instant-read thermometer inserted in the inner thigh registers 165°F; cover the breast with foil if it browns too quickly. Remove the turkey from the oven and let it rest in a warm spot for at least 45 minutes before carving and serving.

chef tips from **jonathan waxman**

ON BRINING Everyone is talking about brining; even my eleven-year-old insists that it's better. Brining is tricky—a little too much and you are left with a salty bird; too little, and it was a waste of time. My sense is, try it and make your own decision.

ON TURNING THE BIRD Turkeys weigh a minimum of 12 pounds, and they are hard objects to maneuver, especially when hot and greasy. Keep things simple by roasting the bird breast side up the whole time and don't bother turning it all.

ON OVEN SPACE Don't crowd the oven with other items: the turkey likes solitary confinement. If you want to roast vegetables with the turkey (like carrots, potatoes and/or turnips), simmer them in turkey stock for 10 minutes and then add them to the roasting pan for the last half hour of roasting.

ON RESTING The turkey should be left in a very warm place to rest. A cold back porch is not good, especially if you have pets or hungry men about.

ON TENTING There's no need to tent your bird when you let it rest (unless you bought it a sleeping bag).

Coriander + Cumin–Crusted Duck Breasts

❝ Duck had always been daunting to me as a home cook. Maybe it's because my favorite restaurant versions seemed so complex, like Daniel Humm's Lavender and Honey Duck at Eleven Madison Park in New York City, or the myriad versions of crispy Peking duck. Then one day at the farmers' market, I saw duck breasts and figured it was time to give the bird another shot. Unlike a whole duck, which takes hours, cooking the breasts takes little more than ten minutes—quite the opposite of a chef-y extravaganza. I air-dried the breasts before cooking them and scored the skin, lessons I learned from Daniel to make it crispy. And I had well-seasoned, juicy duck breasts in the time it takes to sauté chicken. My mistake here? Being intimidated by the unknown. If I can quell my fear of unfamiliar meats, I can try so many things. Next up? Rabbit!

TOTAL TIME: 40 MINUTES   SERVES 4

¼ cup pitted green olives, such as Castelvetrano, finely chopped
3 tablespoons extra-virgin olive oil
1 teaspoon ground coriander
1 teaspoon ground cumin
1 teaspoon kosher salt
Two 1-pound Muscovy duck breasts, patted dry with paper towels, at room temperature

1 Put the olives and olive oil in a small bowl and stir to combine. Set aside.
2 Stir together the coriander, cumin and salt in another small bowl.
3 Using a small sharp knife, carefully score the duck skin in a crosshatch pattern, being sure not to cut into the meat. Rub the spice mixture all over the duck breasts.

4 Put the duck breasts skin side down in a large heavy skillet and turn the heat to medium-low. Cook until the skin is browned and crisp and the fat is rendered, 15 to 20 minutes. Spoon off the fat as the duck cooks (reserve for another use such as cooking potatoes or discard).

5 Carefully turn the duck breasts skin side up and cook over medium heat until just barely firm to the touch and medium-rare within, another 7 to 10 minutes. Transfer the duck breasts to a cutting board and let rest for 10 minutes.

6 Thinly slice the duck breasts crosswise and transfer to a platter. Spoon the olive mixture on top and serve immediately.

chef tips from **daniel humm**

ON THE BEST DUCK BREASTS Use Muscovy duck breasts, which are big and meaty and have less fat under the skin than other types. Rohan ducks are another delicious option.

ON PREPPING THE DUCK Scoring the skin will help render the fat.

ON RENDERING THE FAT It's important to keep draining the fat from the pan as the duck cooks so that it doesn't build up and start cooking the flesh of the breasts.

ON SEASONING VARIATIONS
• Rub duck breasts with ground juniper berries and cloves before cooking.
• Glaze plain cooked duck breasts with a mixture of honey, salt, dried lavender, cumin, coriander and Szechuan peppercorns.
• Glaze with orange juice that's been reduced with star anise and seasoned with salt
• Glaze with hoisin sauce and serve with sliced scallions.

pork shoulder sugo,
page 187

meat

Pork Shoulder Sugo

❝ My good friend Chris is a gentleman farmer. We buy at least half a pig from him every year. After eating our way through the smaller cuts (bacon, ribs, chops) one year, we were left with two pork shoulders—perfect for a party. So I invited about a dozen people to dinner and got started in the kitchen early in the day. I rubbed one shoulder with salt and sugar and roasted it at 300°F for six hours, but the pork never cooked to tender. Not willing to give up, I took the meat out of the oven, cut it up, put it in a pot of tomato sauce and let it cook some more.

Then, frantic, knowing I had to feed a bunch of friends and not certain how the pork shoulder would turn out, I did the only natural thing: I took the second pork shoulder and started all over with a completely different recipe. I made pork *sugo*, slow-roasting the shoulder in a fantastically aromatic tomato sauce at a very low temperature for hours. After an extra two hours in the pot, the first pork shoulder was edible. But the second shoulder was a huge success—falling-apart tender in a sauce that was perfect over pasta. I got lucky this time, but I went to meat master Michael Symon of Lola in Cleveland to get some tips to prevent any future pork fiascoes.

ACTIVE TIME: 30 MINUTES   TOTAL TIME: 6 HOURS   SERVES 8

¼ cup olive oil

2 small yellow onions, finely diced

1 large carrot, peeled and finely diced

8 garlic cloves, finely chopped

Kosher salt and freshly ground black pepper

¼ cup tomato paste

1 tablespoon finely chopped rosemary

1 tablespoon finely chopped thyme

2 cups dry white wine

One 28-ounce can whole peeled tomatoes

One 3-pound boneless pork shoulder roast, trimmed of excess fat

Pasta or polenta and freshly grated Parmigiano-Reggiano, for serving

ON CHOOSING THE PORK As with all ingredients, start with the highest-quality you can afford. I recommend a heritage breed if you can find it. The fattier the pork shoulder, the more flavor it will have and the more tender it'll be.

ON GUARANTEEING TENDER PORK The shoulder has to reach 170°F and hold that temperature for at least 1 hour during cooking. Once this happens, you're guaranteed tender pork, because the intramuscular fat and sinew will have broken down.

ON SALVAGING TOUGH ROAST PORK Remove the pork from the oven and let it cool. Then shred it and cook it down in a tomato sauce for a fantastic ragú.

1 Preheat the oven to 275°F.

2 Heat the olive oil in a large enameled cast-iron casserole over medium-high heat until shimmering. Add the onions, carrot and garlic, season with salt and pepper and cook, stirring, until softened, about 8 minutes. Add the tomato paste and herbs and cook, stirring, until fragrant, about 1 minute. Add the wine, bring to a boil, and cook until the smell of raw alcohol dissipates, about 3 minutes. Add the tomatoes, juices and all, breaking up the tomatoes with a wooden spoon.

3 Nestle the pork in the sauce, sprinkle the top of the roast with salt and pepper and place the casserole in the oven. Roast the pork for 3 hours, or until it's browned on top and the sauce is slightly reduced.

4 Cover the casserole and cook for 2 hours longer, or until the pork is meltingly tender. Remove the pork from the oven and allow it to rest until the meat is cool enough to handle, at least an hour.

5 Remove the meat from the sauce and shred it, discarding any big hunks of fat. Return the shredded meat to the pot. If it seems as if the sauce could use more liquid, add 1 cup of water. Bring the sauce to a boil, then lower the heat to a simmer and cook for 15 minutes to infuse the shredded meat with flavor.

6 Season the sauce with salt and pepper if needed and serve over pasta or polenta, with grated Parmesan on the side.

MAKE AHEAD The sugo is even better made at least 1 day in advance. In fact, you can refrigerate it for up to 5 days; rewarm it over medium-low heat. It also freezes well for up to 1 month.

Pork Tenderloin with Arugula Salsa Verde

> Sometimes a single ingredient can ruin a dish. Take the salsa verde I made to jazz up a straight-ahead pork tenderloin. I whirred the arugula, anchovy, garlic and capers in the food processor, and, as I often do, I asked my fourteen-year-old daughter to taste it for me. You'd think I'd given her fermented whale blubber: she rolled her eyes, she gagged. Finally, she managed one word. "Garlic." Pause. "There's too much garlic." I tried it, and she was right. The recipe called for one garlic clove, and I had used a plump clove from the farmers' market, which turned out to be a lot larger than the average clove. I attempted to neutralize the garlic, piling bread, yogurt, mascarpone, more herbs, oil into the food processor. At the end of all my efforts, the salsa was OK, but definitely not *verde* (the green was muted by all the white add-ins).

I consulted with Ethan Stowell of Staple and Fancy Mercantile in Seattle, who said it's actually near impossible to fix a garlicky salsa verde by adding ingredients. Instead, he recommended making a second batch without any garlic and combining it with the first. To make sure you don't repeat my mistake, I've given a precise measurement for the garlic below instead of calling for a single clove.

ACTIVE TIME: 20 MINUTES   TOTAL TIME: 45 MINUTES   SERVES 6

2 pork tenderloins (about 1¼ pounds each), patted dry with
   paper towels

½ cup extra-virgin olive oil, divided

Kosher salt and freshly ground black pepper

¼ cup capers, drained

¾ teaspoon minced garlic

4 anchovy fillets

Large pinch of crushed red pepper, or more to taste

2 packed cups baby arugula

1 tablespoon Dijon mustard

1 tablespoon red wine vinegar

1 Preheat the oven to 400°F.

2 Heat a large heavy ovenproof skillet over medium-high heat. Rub the pork tenderloins with 3 tablespoons of the olive oil. Season them liberally with salt and black pepper. Put them in the hot skillet and cook until well browned on the bottom, about 3 minutes.

3 Turn the pork tenderloins over and transfer the skillet to the oven. Roast until an instant-read thermometer inserted into the thickest part of the pork registers 145°F (or until the pork is firm to the touch), about 15 minutes.

4 Meanwhile, put the capers, garlic, anchovies and crushed red pepper in the bowl of a food processor and pulse to combine. Add the arugula and pulse until finely chopped.

5 Add the mustard, vinegar and the remaining ¼ cup plus 1 tablespoon of olive oil and pulse until a coarse puree forms. Transfer the salsa verde to a bowl, season to taste with salt and crushed red pepper if needed and set aside.

6 Transfer the pork to a cutting board and allow it to rest for 10 minutes, then cut it into thick slices. Transfer the slices to a platter, spoon over the salsa verde and serve immediately.

SERVE WITH Spicy Greens Caesar Salad (page 45).

WHY DIDN'T I THINK OF THAT?
MORE RECIPE IDEAS FROM ETHAN STOWELL

- Add chopped hard-boiled eggs and cornichons to turn your salsa verde into a sauce gribiche.
- Add an herb (or a few different herbs) to or in place of the arugula. A mint salsa verde (leave out the garlic) will be more sweet; arugula mixed with parsley and basil is more savory.
- Salsa verde is great with anything charred, like grilled salmon, whole roasted fish or grilled bread. The bright fresh flavors really complement the deep, strong tones of charred food.

chef tips from **ethan stowell**

ON GARLIC Avoid prepeeled garlic. And use only a small amount of garlic in the salsa verde, as the flavor will get stronger as it sits.

ON PUREEING GREENS Pulse greens quickly, or the food processor can overheat and "cook" them, and you'll lose the vibrancy of your sauce.

Pork Chops with Five-Minute Umami Sauce

66 When I was first learning to cook, I focused my energy on American-Italian-French flavors, because those were the ones I loved and knew best. And then came miso. When miso turned up in supermarkets, I instantly became enamored of it, adding it to everything from soups and stews to sauces and vinaigrettes. It's like putting on a 4-carat diamond ring when you're dressed in jeans and a T-shirt. Proving that point, when I served pork chops with this miso pan sauce one Sunday night, my husband, Barclay, looked up after his first bite and said, "Wow. This is the best pork chop ever." Since I don't want to do *everything* with miso, I asked one of the greatest meat cooks in the world, Bobby Flay, to give me some suggestions for what else to do with pork chops. His inspiring answers are on the following page.

TOTAL TIME: 30 MINUTES   SERVES 4

Four 1-inch-thick bone-in pork rib chops (about ³⁄₄ pound each), at room temperature
Kosher salt and freshly ground black pepper
2 tablespoons vegetable oil
1¹⁄₂ teaspoons finely grated ginger (preferably grated on a microplane), juice reserved
2 teaspoons freshly squeezed lime juice
1¹⁄₂ teaspoons agave nectar
¹⁄₂ teaspoon rice vinegar
1 tablespoon red miso
¹⁄₄ cup water
3 tablespoons unsalted cold butter, diced
2 tablespoons roughly chopped cilantro, for garnish

1 Preheat the oven to 400°F.

2 Season both sides of the pork chops evenly and liberally with salt and pepper.

3 Divide the oil between two large heavy ovenproof skillets (ideally cast-iron or stainless steel) and heat over high heat. When the oil is nearly smoking, carefully place the pork chops in the skillets and cook until well browned on the bottom, 3 to 4 minutes.

4 Flip the chops, transfer the skillets to the oven and roast for about 7 minutes, until the chops are firm to the touch and an instant-read thermometer inserted into the thickest part registers 145°F. Transfer the chops to a plate or board and let rest for a few minutes while you make the sauce.

5 Whisk the ginger and its juice with the lime juice, agave and rice vinegar in a small bowl. Whisk the miso with the water in a small saucepan over medium-high heat until combined and hot; do not boil. Whisk in the butter cube by cube until melted and smooth. Whisk in the ginger mixture and cook, until the sauce is smooth and hot, about 1 minute. Remove from the heat.

6 Transfer the pork chops to plates or a platter, drizzle with the sauce and garnish with the cilantro. Serve immediately.

MAKE AHEAD The sauce can be refrigerated for up to 1 week. Rewarm it over low heat, whisking. If the sauce separates, simply whisk in cold water a teaspoon at a time until it comes back together.

WHY DIDN'T I THINK OF THAT?
MORE RECIPE IDEAS FROM BOBBY FLAY

- Pork chops and applesauce remind me vividly of my childhood. I often reach for the almighty apple when cooking a pork chop. I'll make a spicy apple chutney spiked with fresh ginger and orange zest or a double apple butter with green chiles and cinnamon.
- Lately at my restaurant Gato I've been pairing porterhouse-cut pork chops with a tomatoey, almost osso buco–like sauce and a gremolata with lemon and orange.
- No matter what the flavor profile, I like my pork chops charred or crusted on a grill or in a cast-iron pan with a spice rub cooked into them on one side. I then finish them slowly to medium doneness by turning down the heat on the stovetop or putting them in a 400°F oven.

Jerk Lamb

" About ten years ago, I was changing my son's diaper and my mother was waiting in the kitchen for me to finish cooking dinner, when the lamb in the oven caught on fire—the fat had flared up, hit the broiler coils and burst into flames. My mother, the consummate noncook, was amused (she'd never expected me to actually know how to cook and this proved it!) and alarmed. I was mortified. The lamb was both burnt and severely undercooked, which is to say, inedible. My mother subsists on Hershey bars, so she didn't mind in the least. She had a ready-to-eat meal in her handbag, and a story to tell forever.

Zak Pelaccio, chef of Fish & Game in Hudson, New York, assured me that if I ever wanted to try this again, I could avoid flames, and the fallout, if I placed the meat on a wire rack set on the baking sheet to allow the fat to drip off the meat. Or I could simply lower the oven rack so the meat wasn't as close to the flame or coil. This recipe is based on one from Paul Chung, an accomplished self-taught cook who grew up in Jamaica and used to work in the *Food & Wine* mailroom. Cooked properly, it is one of my favorite fast, feed-a-crowd dishes. It's spicy from the black pepper and chiles, and it also has a warm heat from the allspice.

TOTAL TIME: 30 MINUTES + AT LEAST 8 HOURS MARINATING
SERVES 12

....

1 large red onion, roughly chopped

4 garlic cloves, chopped

2 jalapeños or 1 habanero, stemmed and roughly chopped (seeds and all)

1 tablespoon five-spice powder

1 tablespoon ground allspice

1 tablespoon freshly ground black pepper

1 teaspoon freshly grated nutmeg

1 tablespoon dried thyme

1 teaspoon kosher salt

¼ cup soy sauce

2 tablespoons apple cider vinegar

2 tablespoons canola oil

1 butterflied leg of lamb (approximately 7 pounds), trimmed of excess fat and cut crosswise in half

ON FAT When broiling meat, always pay attention to how much fat is in the pan or on the item you're broiling. If there is a lot of fat, lower your oven rack so the meat is not as close to the flame or coil.

ON THE ROASTING SETUP For more drip and less splatter, set the meat on a wire rack on a baking sheet or use a broiling pan with a perforated insert.

ON BROILING ALTERNATIVES You can also grill the lamb, or sear it in a cast-iron pan, and then finish cooking it in a 400°F oven.

1   Put the onion, garlic, chile, spices, thyme and salt into the bowl of a food processor and pulse to a coarse paste. With the machine running, drizzle in the soy sauce, vinegar and oil.

2   Put each piece of lamb in a 1-gallon resealable bag. Divide the marinade between the bags, seal the bags and turn to coat the lamb well. Refrigerate for at least 8 hours, and up to 24 hours.

3   When ready to cook the lamb, bring it to room temperature. Line a baking sheet with foil and set a wire rack on top. Preheat your broiler to high.

4   Remove one piece of lamb from the bag, allowing the excess marinade to drip off, place it on the prepared baking sheet and broil about 4 inches from the heat for 10 minutes, until browned in spots and sizzling. Flip the lamb and broil for 8 to 10 minutes longer, until it is browned and an instant-read thermometer inserted into the thickest part registers 125°F. Transfer the lamb to a cutting board and allow it to rest for at least 10 minutes. Meanwhile, broil the other piece of lamb.

5   Thinly slice the lamb across the grain. Transfer to a platter and serve immediately.

NOTE   The spice rub is also terrific on chicken or fish.

MAKE AHEAD   The marinade can be stored in an airtight container in the refrigerator for up to a week.

WHY DIDN'T I THINK OF THAT?
MORE RECIPE IDEAS FROM ZAK PELACCIO

- Marinate the lamb in a mixture of minced garlic and chiles, sunflower oil, white wine, and rosemary. After you cook it, sprinkle the meat with wine vinegar.
- Marinate the lamb with a paste made from minced garlic cloves, minced shallots, ground coriander, freshly ground white pepper and sea salt, ground fennel seeds, crushed cardamon pods and crushed dried cayenne chiles, mixed with some grapeseed oil and fish sauce.

Grilled Skirt Steak with Asian Chimichurri

" I often experiment with recipes when I'm having a dinner party, and sometimes that doesn't produce the best result. I was making skirt steak with an Asian chimichurri sauce, and half an hour before the meat was supposed to go on the grill, I decided to marinate it in chimichurri in addition to serving it alongside. But just as I was about to put the steaks on the grill, I got nervous. What if the herbs burned? What if this was a bad idea? Not wanting to ruin dinner for eight, I called *Top Chef* winner Kristen Kish. She assured me that the herbs wouldn't burn, but she recommended that I pat the beef dry.

The steak was fine, but didn't seem have to benefited at all from its brief chimichurri soak. Kristen wasn't surprised: to absorb the flavors, the steak would have needed to marinate for at least an hour, she said. As cooking experiments go, this one was a draw. This recipe was just fine without marinating. Chimichurri as a sauce is all you need to make this a terrific, flavorful dish.

TOTAL TIME: 40 MINUTES   SERVES 4

....

¾ cup cilantro leaves, finely chopped

¼ cup celery leaves, finely chopped

1 tablespoon minced peeled ginger

2 teaspoons soy sauce

¼ cup plus 2 tablespoons olive oil

2 pounds skirt steak, membranes trimmed

1 teaspoon kosher salt

1 Put the cilantro, celery leaves, ginger and soy sauce in a small bowl, add ¼ cup of the olive oil and stir to combine. Set aside.

2 Prepare a fire in a charcoal grill or preheat a gas grill to high. Alternatively, set a heavy grill pan over high heat.

3 Rub the skirt steak with the remaining 2 tablespoons of olive oil and sprinkle evenly on both sides with the salt. Place the steak on the grill and cook until browned on the first side, about 4 minutes. Turn the steak and cook until browned on the second side and cooked, medium to medium-rare, about 4 minutes. (Exact cooking times will vary depending on the thickness of the skirt steak.)

4 Transfer the steak to a cutting board and let it rest for at least 10 minutes before slicing it against the grain. Serve with the chimichurri.

Korean Meat Loaf

" The meat loaf drama happened on a Friday night after a very busy week at work. I'd signed up to bring three Korean-style dishes to a potluck dinner at my friend Cheryl's house. Inspired by some of the great Korean-American innovators, like Edward Lee of 610 Magnolia in Louisville, Kentucky, I planned to make Korean Meat Loaf, Quickest Cucumber Kimchi (page 65) and Napa Cabbage Slaw (page 55). This seemed reasonable, since each dish required little more than chopping and measuring. Cheryl had coordinated the entire menu around my Asian choices. I got home at 6 p.m., far later than I'd expected, and the race against time began.

I roped my friend Jacque and my daughter, Sylvie, into being prep cooks, urging them to chop, chop, chop. And then I committed a critical mistake with the meat loaf, one I could have so easily avoided: I didn't read my recipe notes through to the end. Talk about a rookie error. I thought the meat loaf cooked in twenty-five minutes, but it actually needed almost triple that. In a panic, I threw the ingredients together as quickly as possible. I formed them into a loaf on a baking sheet and spread the incredibly tasty *gochujang*-ketchup combo on top. In the end, I still didn't have enough time. So I took the meat loaf out of the oven and brought it half-baked to Cheryl's. As fate would have it, I was the only one at the potluck who needed the oven to finish a dish, and the meat loaf got the extra time it needed.

ACTIVE TIME: 30 MINUTES   TOTAL TIME: 1 HOUR AND 50 MINUTES
SERVES 6 TO 8

....

1 cup *gochujang* (Korean chile paste)

1 cup ketchup

4 teaspoons minced peeled ginger, divided

6 garlic cloves, minced, divided

3 large eggs

8 scallions, very finely chopped

1 cup finely chopped kimchi, drained well

1½ teaspoons kosher salt

1 teaspoon Asian sesame oil

2 teaspoons soy sauce

1 cup panko bread crumbs

1 pound ground beef (80% lean)

1 pound ground pork

1 Preheat the oven to 375°F. Line a rimmed baking sheet with parchment paper.

2 Whisk together the *gochujang* and ketchup with 1 teaspoon of the ginger and ½ teaspoon of the garlic in a small bowl. Set aside.

3 Whisk the eggs thoroughly in a large bowl. Add the remaining garlic and ginger, the scallions, kimchi, salt, sesame oil and soy sauce and stir until thoroughly combined. Add the bread crumbs, ground beef and ground pork and lightly mix everything with your hands; don't overwork the mixture.

4 Transfer the meat mixture to the prepared baking sheet and shape it into a rectangular loaf measuring roughly 9 by 5 inches. Spread ⅓ cup of the *gochujang* mixture on top of it. Transfer the meat loaf to the oven and bake until it is firm to the touch and an instant-read thermometer inserted in the center registers 165°F, about 1 hour and 10 minutes. Let the meat loaf rest for at least 15 minutes before slicing. Serve with the remaining *gochujang* sauce alongside.

MAKE AHEAD The meat mixture and the *gochujang* sauce can be refrigerated (separately) for up to 1 day.

WHY DIDN'T I THINK OF THAT?
MORE RECIPE IDEAS FROM EDWARD LEE

- Make a simple vinaigrette with *gochujang* thinned with lemon juice, rice vinegar, a little honey and sesame oil to flavor anything from hearty salads to raw fish.
- Add a tablespoon of *gochujang* to chicken broth, along with a little soy sauce, and it will elevate your soup to a spicy, earthy, umami-rich bowl of goodness.
- Fry some bacon in a pan. Once it's crispy, add a spoonful of *gochujang* to the pan, mixing it into the rendered fat. Add a little soy sauce and brown sugar and cook the bacon in the sauce until it reduces and coats the bacon. Serve with sunny-side-up eggs and toast, and spoon a little of the sauce over the eggs. A breakfast worth waking up early for.

chef tips from edward lee

ON FORMING THE MEAT LOAF
Don't overwork the meat mixture—that guarantees a dense meat loaf. Mix the ingredients just enough to distribute the flavors evenly. Don't be tempted to "squeeze" the meat. And don't pack the meat when shaping it—work gently.

ON *GOCHUJANG* The distinctive quality of this chile paste is its fermented flavor. For a good substitute, add your favorite hot sauce—Sriracha works well— to some dark miso along with some cayenne pepper and a pinch of sugar.

Steak au Poivre

66 I hadn't cooked for just my husband in fourteen years. I'd fed him, of course. Hosted dinner parties with him. Made his coffee and fried a few eggs in the morning. But I hadn't really made a romantic dinner for two since before our first child was born. With the kids at camp, I decided to make his favorite meal, steak au poivre: a New York strip steak crusted in crunchy crushed peppercorns with a flamed Cognac and mustard sauce. My biggest fear was that I would set my kitchen on fire. I held my breath as I struck a teeny wooden matchstick to light the Cognac. That went well! The flames eventually died down, and I proceeded with the rest of the recipe. Disaster was averted, or so I thought, until we tasted the steaks. The sauce had a bitter, astringent edge.

Alex Guarnaschelli, of the New York City restaurant Butter, identified my mistake: cooking in a cast-iron pan. As she explained to me, if you're making a pan sauce that has acid in it, you need to use a nonreactive pan.

TOTAL TIME: 30 MINUTES + 30 MINUTES TO BRING STEAKS TO ROOM TEMPERATURE   SERVES 2

1½ tablespoons black peppercorns

Two 1-inch-thick New York strip steaks (about ½ pound each), excess fat trimmed, at room temperature

Kosher salt

2 tablespoons vegetable or canola oil

¼ cup Cognac

2 small shallots, grated to a paste (preferably on a microplane)

1 tablespoon plus 1 teaspoon Dijon mustard

¼ cup crème fraîche

¼ cup freshly squeezed lemon juice

¼ cup water

2 tablespoons finely chopped flat-leaf parsley

1 teaspoon grated lemon zest

1 Put the peppercorns on a small rimmed baking sheet and crush them with a small heavy skillet; be sure not to bash them. Season each side of the steaks generously with salt, then mop up the crushed peppercorns with both sides of the steaks.

2 Heat a large heavy stainless steel skillet over high heat. Add the oil and swirl to coat the bottom of the skillet. When the oil is smoking hot, carefully place the steaks in the skillet, laying them down away from you (so that if any hot fat splatters, it splatters away from you). Let the steaks cook until the underside is nicely browned and they don't resist when you try to flip them, about 4 minutes. Turn and cook on the second side until well browned, another 3 to 4 minutes. Turn the steaks onto their fat edges and brown them until the fat is nice and crisp, about 2 minutes. Transfer the steaks to a serving dish or dinner plates and let them rest while you make the sauce.

3 Pour off and discard all but a very thin layer of fat from the skillet. Take the skillet off the heat and add the Cognac. Carefully return the skillet to the heat—the alcohol should immediately burst into flames (not a bad thing!); if it doesn't, ignite the Cognac with a long match or lighter. Once the flames have subsided, lower the heat to medium, add the shallots and a pinch of salt and cook, stirring, until the raw shallot aroma disappears, about a minute. Whisk in the mustard, crème fraîche, lemon juice and water. Season the sauce to taste with salt, and add more water if you prefer a looser consistency. Remove from the heat.

4 Whisk half the parsley into the sauce and sprinkle the steaks with the remaining parsley. Season each steak with a pinch more salt and scatter the lemon zest evenly on top. Spoon the sauce over the steaks and serve immediately.

chef tips from **alex guarnaschelli**

ON PANS When making a pan sauce, acid is boss over cookware. You can use cast-iron for the steak, but not for the sauce. Nonstick pans for steak? No way.

ON CRUSHING THE PEPPERCORNS Crush them with a small heavy skillet (don't bash them): Focus your weight in the middle of the pan, and push down and forward. Imagine you're smearing peanut butter on toast. Focus some love on the areas that didn't get too crushed. Then use the steaks to mop up the remaining peppercorns as if you're sponging down a counter.

ON GETTING A GOOD CRUST ON THE STEAK When the crust is terrific and browned and it releases itself—these are built-in visual indicators

that tell you the steak is ready to flip. If you notice a spot that isn't too browned, tilt the pan so all the fat collects at the bottom and use a spoon to scoop up the fat and baste that spot—go right over that spot as if you're filling in a blank.

ON MAKING THE PAN SAUCE Evaluate how much fat you have in the pan. You might need to pour some off—you don't want your sauce to just taste like fat. As chef Larry Forgione told me twenty-some years ago, you can always put it back in, but you can't take it out. Also, the more hot grease in your sauce, the more likely it is to separate. To thicken the sauce, add grated shallots, which give flavor and vegetal body to the sauce. Mustard is a natural thickener too.

ON FLAMBÉING Take the pan off the heat to add the alcohol, then put it back on the flame—you don't want to risk getting flames rising up into the bottle or anything superscary like that.

ON GARNISHING Add a bit of parsley. You always need a little acid and a little grass. My biggest advice on finishing dishes, though, is to Coco Chanel your food: Take one or two things out before the dish leaves the kitchen. Less is more.

Great Ribs

" Here's where I have to admit that I'm often a lazy cook. I avoid recipes that seem like too much work. Until recently, ribs fell squarely into this camp. Much as I loved them, I didn't feel they were worth the effort. They needed basting. They needed turning. They needed attention. But then I found out about a recipe where the ribs are simmered until tender and then finished under the broiler, and all of a sudden, making ribs seemed manageable. Plus, the flavor-packed cooking liquid becomes the finishing sauce. Another great trick for a lazy cook.

ACTIVE TIME: 30 MINUTES   TOTAL TIME: 2½ HOURS   SERVES 8

6 garlic cloves, minced
One 2-inch piece of ginger, peeled and minced
1 teaspoon crushed red pepper
½ cup soy sauce
½ cup hoisin sauce
¼ cup honey
¼ cup apple cider vinegar, or more to taste
6 pounds pork baby back ribs, cut between the bones into
    individual ribs (about 3 dozen ribs)

1 Put the garlic, ginger, crushed red pepper, soy sauce, hoisin, honey and vinegar in a very large pot and bring to a boil. Add the ribs and stir to coat with the liquid. Add enough water to cover the ribs and bring to a boil, then reduce the heat to medium-low and cover the pot. Simmer the ribs, uncovering the pot to stir them every so often, until the meat is very tender, about 1½ hours.

2 Line a rimmed baking sheet with foil. Using a slotted spoon, transfer the ribs to the baking sheet. Set aside.

3 Bring the cooking liquid back to a boil and cook until the sauce is as thick as barbecue sauce, about 20 minutes. Season the sauce with a bit more vinegar if you like. Remove from the heat.

4 Preheat the broiler. Brush the ribs with half of the sauce and broil until the sauce bubbles, 2 to 5 minutes, depending on the strength of your broiler. Remove the ribs from the broiler, carefully turn them over and brush with the remaining sauce. Broil until the sauce bubbles and lacquers the ribs, another couple of minutes.

5 Transfer the ribs to a platter, drizzle over any sauce that's on the baking sheet and serve immediately.

SERVE WITH Napa Cabbage Slaw (page 41).

Mushroom + Beef Stew

" The hunks of beef for the stew were the most gorgeous red when I took them out of the butcher's paper. I felt a huge surge of pride at securing such beautiful meat—I had snagged it from my friend Chris. It was meat from his own cows. As I tipped the meat into the pot of shimmering oil, I felt a buzz of happiness. I shook the juices that had collected in the paper into the pot. I didn't want to waste anything! My happiness, though, faded as that red meat slowly turned gray. Instead of searing the meat, I had braised it. I made a big mistake by adding liquid to the pot as the meat was browning. Though the stew's rich, mushroomy sauce masked my error, the beef lacked a special hearty roastiness. I felt like I'd let down that animal—and my friend the gentleman farmer.

Now I know to keep beef as dry as possible when it goes in the pot. I've also amped up the mushrooms for the stew and held back on the beef, making this a somewhat lighter but supersatisfying winter dish. Star chef Daniel Boulud, who is a whiz with one-pot meals, gave me some additional suggestions.

ACTIVE TIME: 45 MINUTES   TOTAL TIME: 2¼ HOURS   SERVES 8

¼ cup plus 2 tablespoons olive oil

2 pounds trimmed flatiron steak or beef stew meat, cut into 1-inch pieces and patted dry with paper towels

Kosher salt and freshly ground black pepper

3 pounds mushrooms (a mix of cremini and shiitake is great), stems reserved for another use, caps halved or quartered if large

1 large yellow onion, halved lengthwise and thinly sliced

3 garlic cloves, minced

2 tablespoons all-purpose flour

¼ cup tomato paste

1 bottle (750 ml) dry red wine, such as Merlot or Côtes du Rhône

2 dried shiitake or porcini mushrooms

1 tablespoon Dijon mustard

1 tablespoon soy sauce

½ cup lightly packed flat-leaf parsley leaves, finely chopped

1 tablespoon finely grated lemon zest

Egg noodles, potatoes or rice, for serving

1 Heat 2 tablespoons of the olive oil in a large heavy pot over medium-high heat. Season the beef liberally with salt and pepper. Add half of the beef to the pot and cook, turning occasionally, until well browned, about 8 minutes. Using a slotted spoon, transfer the beef to a plate. Repeat with the remaining beef, and transfer it to the plate.

2 Pour off all the fat from the pot. Add 2 tablespoons of the olive oil and half of the fresh mushrooms to the pot and cook over medium-high heat, stirring occasionally, until the mushrooms release their liquid, the liquid evaporates and the mushrooms brown, about 8 minutes. Transfer the mushrooms to their own plate. Repeat with the remaining 2 tablespoons olive oil and remaining mushrooms; add to the plate.

3 Add the onions, garlic and a pinch each of salt and pepper to the pot and cook over medium heat, stirring occasionally, until the onions are softened and beginning to brown, about 8 minutes.

4 Add the flour and tomato paste and cook, stirring, until the pot is quite dry, about 2 minutes. Add the wine, turn the heat to high and bring to a boil.

5 Lower the heat to a simmer, return the beef to the pot and add the dried mushrooms. Cover the pot and simmer the stew, giving it a stir occasionally, until the meat is tender, about 1½ hours. Remove and discard the dried mushrooms.

6 Stir the reserved sautéed mushrooms, the mustard and the soy sauce into the stew and season to taste with salt and pepper.

7 Mix together the parsley and lemon zest in a small bowl. Serve the stew with egg noodles, potatoes or rice, sprinkling each portion with a little of the parsley mixture.

MAKE AHEAD The stew is best made a day in advance. In fact, you can make it up to 4 days in advance; rewarm it over medium-low heat. It also freezes well for up to 3 months.

chef tips from
daniel boulud

ON BEEF The best cut of beef for stew is flatiron steak, cut from the shoulder. Trim excess fat from the beef so that your stew doesn't become greasy.

ON MUSHROOMS To prep a lot of mushrooms at once, put them in a bowl of cold water, stir and let the dirt settle to the bottom, then lift the mushrooms from the water. If needed, repeat. Then spread the mushrooms on a towel-lined tray to dry before cooking.

ON TEXTURE If your stew is too thin, puree some of the cooking liquid and vegetables in a blender, then stir it back into the stew.

CHEF VARIATIONS
- To give the stew extra body, add a piece of calf's foot or pork belly skin, both of which have a lot of collagen.
- Finish the stew with a splash of flavored oil, vinegar or crème fraîche or sour cream.
- Serve the stew with garnishes such as mustard, horseradish or pickled vegetables.
- If your stew seems too acidic or strong, you can add a citrus marmalade or chopped chocolate to give it a little *je ne sais quoi*.

lemon-pepper whole trout,
page 162

seafood

lemon-pepper whole trout · 162

halibut with red coconut curry · 165

sole with pecorino-and-parsley crumbs · 167

roasted salmon with mustard + panko · 168

swordfish kebabs with chermoula · 171

mexico city shrimp · 174

seared scallops with fennel + citrus salad · 177

pan-roasted lobster with red miso + citrus sauce · 179

clams with garlic, ginger + sriracha · 185

squid with chorizo + pickled jalapeños · 186

Lemon-Pepper Whole Trout

" Having been convinced of the virtue of nose-to-tail cooking by bearded Brooklynites and various chef friends, but knowing that I wasn't ready to take on a whole pig, I decided to conquer cooking a whole fish. I bought a few small trout from a sustainable farm near our house in upstate New York. I seasoned and seared them, then turned the heat down to slowly finish cooking them. Even with this well-thought-out approach though, they were overcooked and flavorless.

John Besh, of August in New Orleans, has been catching and preparing fish his whole life. He applauded the choice of trout for my first attempt at cooking a whole fish: because of its diminutive size, it's the perfect fish to panfry. This empowered me to try again. In order to add more flavor, I made slits in the skin of the trout and brushed on some lemon-pepper olive oil. And I followed John's tip for determining when the fish was done—I wiggled the dorsal fin at the top of the fish, and when it came out cleanly, I knew it was ready. Now that I've conquered this dish, I'll have to take another tip from John and start by catching the fish.

TOTAL TIME: 25 MINUTES   SERVES 4

¼ cup extra-virgin olive oil, divided
1 teaspoon finely grated lemon zest
Kosher salt and freshly ground black pepper
2 whole trout, cleaned and patted dry with paper towels
½ lemon, thinly sliced
1 garlic clove, thinly sliced
A few sprigs of whatever herbs you have on hand,
   such as oregano or thyme

1 Whisk 2 tablespoons of the olive oil with the lemon zest and ½ teaspoon each salt and pepper in a small bowl.

2 Score the skin on both sides of each fish in three spots, being careful not to cut all the way down to the bone—just a few shallow slashes. Season the inside of each fish with salt and pepper. Brush the outside of each trout with half the lemon-pepper oil, rubbing it into the slits. Fill the cavities of the trout with the lemon and garlic slices and herbs.

3 Heat the remaining 2 tablespoons of olive oil in a large cast-iron skillet over medium-high heat until shimmering. Carefully place the trout in the hot pan and cook, undisturbed, until their undersides are nicely browned and crisp, about 6 minutes. Using a spatula, carefully flip the fish over and cook until the second side is nicely browned and the fish is just cooked through, another 4 to 6 minutes.

4 Transfer the trout to a platter or plates and serve immediately.

NOTE The trout goes well with just about any side dish, but Spiced Creamed Spinach (page 74) is particularly nice.

chef tips from **john besh**

ON PANFRYING TROUT Trout is the easiest fish to panfry whole because it's small.

ON THE BEST PAN FOR WHOLE FISH When cooking whole fish, it's all about heat retention and avoiding hot spots in the pan, so the heavier the pan, the better. Nothing beats a cast-iron skillet or a copper pan.

ON THE IMPORTANCE OF A WELL-SEASONED PAN If you use a cast-iron pan, make sure it is well seasoned, and therefore almost nonstick, so that you can flip the fish over more easily.

ON CHECKING FOR DONENESS To see if the fish is done, test the flesh near the dorsal fin (the fin on the back)—it should easily come away from the bone.

ON CRIMES AGAINST TROUT There's a tendency to think that more is better—more seasoning, more heat—but overcooking trout's delicate flesh is the biggest crime you can commit.

ON GETTING A CRISP CRUST To get a bit of a crust on your fish, dust it with Wondra flour before cooking.

ON THE BEST SAUCE FOR TROUT Dress pan-seared trout with positively the best combination ever invented: brown butter, salt and a squeeze of Meyer lemon.

Halibut with Red Coconut Curry

66 When I cook, not surprisingly, I often turn to a recipe that we've published in *Food & Wine*. So it now seems the height of perversity that I chose a random recipe from the web when I had Tina Ujlaki, the magazine's executive food editor, over for dinner. I'd chosen a "healthy" recipe that looked OK until I started cooking. I used "lite" coconut milk, so the curry was thin. It also lacked both sweetness and acidity. It was a fantastic, though unfortunate, reminder of the importance of using trusted recipe sources. Instead of impressing Tina with my prowess, I had to call upon her expertise to help fix that miserable dish—something she does all day long at work. We added full-fat coconut milk, increased the aromatics and doubled the red curry paste. Here is the tweaked dish, which is quite delicious, but no longer low-cal. I was lucky to have Tina in the kitchen with me that night, but I wanted to make sure the mistake didn't happen again, so I got in touch with chef Bryant Ng of Cassia in Los Angeles, who specializes in Southeast Asian cooking and provided the Chef Tips on the following page.

TOTAL TIME: 40 MINUTES   SERVES 6

2 tablespoons canola oil
4 medium shallots, finely chopped
2 tablespoons minced peeled ginger
4 garlic cloves, minced
¼ cup Thai red curry paste
One 13.5-ounce can full-fat unsweetened coconut milk
1 cup chicken stock or low-sodium chicken broth
Kosher salt
Six 6-ounce skinless halibut fillets, patted dry with paper towels
2 scallions, thinly sliced
½ cup chopped cilantro
Steamed white rice and lime wedges, for serving

1 Put the oil in a large skillet set over medium heat, add the shallots, ginger and garlic and cook, stirring occasionally, until softened and just barely beginning to brown, about 5 minutes.
2 Add the curry paste and cook, stirring, until the aroma from the skillet is wonderfully fragrant, about 3 minutes.

3 Whisk in the coconut milk, stock and a generous pinch of salt and bring to a boil over high heat. Cook the sauce over medium-high heat until slightly thickened, 3 to 5 minutes.

4 Turn the heat to medium-low and gently place the halibut fillets in the pan in a single layer. Place a lid on the pan and let the fish simmer, turning once, until it flakes easily when prodded with a fork or a knife, about 5 minutes.

5 Using a thin, flexible spatula, transfer the fish to shallow bowls. Spoon the curry sauce over the fish. Scatter the scallions and cilantro on top and serve with rice and lime wedges.

MAKE AHEAD The sauce can be refrigerated for up to 1 week.

chef tips from **bryant ng**

ON CURRY PASTE VERSUS POWDER Curry pastes tend to be better than curry powders because they have more depth of flavor. When purchasing one, price is a good indicator of quality. Pastes from Thailand or Malaysia are best.

ON RED VERSUS GREEN CURRY The difference between red and green curry lies in the chiles—green chiles versus red chiles. They can be used interchangeably, but green curry is usually spicier than red.

ON SEASONING CURRY Balance is key in a great curry. Should it be sweeter? Should it have a touch of acid? Should it have a more savory profile? With seafood, finish it with a bit of acid (coconut vinegar or a squeeze of lime) to brighten the curry and to highlight the seafood.

ON SPICINESS Take spiciness into account when balancing the flavors. When used in moderation, hot chiles make you salivate and heighten your perception of the other tastes. Taken to a higher Scoville level, spiciness dulls the senses, but it can give you an endorphin high, which is an experience all its own. Ain't nothing like a high high!

ON DOCTORING MILD CURRY If your curry is too mild, add a little ground dried chile (use a clean-flavored one like chile de árbol). It will add heat without significantly altering the flavor. If your curry is too spicy, just drink lots of alcohol!

ON OTHER USES FOR CURRY PASTE
• Use curry paste as a marinade. Loosen it with coconut milk and season to taste with salt and sugar. Rub the marinade on meats, poultry, seafood or vegetables and grill.
• Add a little curry paste to bread dough to give it distinctive character.
• Incorporate curry paste in the crust for chicken potpie

Sole with Pecorino-and-Parsley Crumbs

" This was the first recipe that made me feel that I could maybe, possibly, become a decent cook. Why? I prepared fish, which is notoriously tricky for beginners, and I didn't mess it up. That's because the recipe, based on a favorite from the brilliant British cook Nigel Slater, is so simple. All you need to do is place a fillet of sole on a baking sheet, cover it with herbed bread crumbs, put it in the oven (you could even do this in the toaster oven) and then take it out after 10 to 15 minutes. If you want even more flavor, you can add spices such as coriander or cumin to the bread crumbs, but it's unnecessary. This is pretty perfect just the way it is.

ACTIVE TIME: 10 MINUTES   TOTAL TIME: 25 MINUTES   SERVES 4

¼ cup finely grated Pecorino cheese
¼ cup finely chopped flat-leaf parsley
¼ cup panko bread crumbs
¼ cup extra-virgin olive oil
½ teaspoon kosher salt, plus more to taste
½ teaspoon freshly ground black pepper, plus more to taste
Four 6-ounce lemon sole fillets

1 Preheat the oven to 450°F. Line a baking sheet with parchment paper.
2 Stir together the cheese, parsley, bread crumbs, olive oil and ½ teaspoon each salt and pepper in a small bowl.
3 Lay the sole fillets on the prepared baking sheet and season them with salt and pepper. Sprinkle the Pecorino crumbs evenly over the fish and gently pat them down to help them adhere.
4 Roast until the topping is golden brown and the fish is almost opaque when tested with a paring knife, about 7 minutes. Transfer to plates and serve immediately.

Roasted Salmon with Mustard + Panko

> I don't really understand the desire to impress people with a fancy meal, but maybe that's because I'm so consumed by my fear of disappointing them. This concern has led me to develop some foolproof recipes, like this salmon that's rubbed with mustard, coated with a panko crust and roasted. What I've learned from cooking this often is that you need to make sure that the thin end of the salmon doesn't overcook as the thicker part cooks to perfection. As my guests have a glass of wine and some hors d'oeuvres, I linger by the oven, keeping tabs on the fish's progress. When I put the fish on a platter, all crispy and browned on top, my fear is replaced by a quiet pride.

ACTIVE TIME: 5 MINUTES   TOTAL TIME: 25 MINUTES   SERVES 8

3 tablespoons olive oil, divided
One 3-pound skin-on center-cut fillet or side of salmon
Kosher salt
½ cup Dijon mustard
1¼ cups panko bread crumbs

1 Preheat the oven to 425°F. Line a baking sheet with foil. Drizzle 1 tablespoon of the olive oil on the foil and use your fingers to rub it over the surface.

2 Place the salmon on the foil, skin side down, and sprinkle evenly with a large pinch of salt. Spread the mustard evenly over the top of the salmon.

3 Put the remaining 2 tablespoons of olive oil in a small bowl and add the panko and a pinch of salt. Stir until the crumbs are evenly moistened, then pack them on top of the salmon.

4 Roast the fish until the bread crumbs are nicely browned and the blade of a dinner knife inserted into the thickest part of the salmon is hot to the touch, 18 to 20 minutes.

5 Cut the salmon into individual portions and serve.

Swordfish Kebabs with Chermoula

" After courageously volunteering to cook for my pal Cheryl's colleagues and friends, I chose my dish carefully. I landed on swordfish in a chermoula marinade that doubles as a sauce, a Moroccan-inspired dish based on a recipe by Tamara Murphy of Brasa in Seattle. I plattered up the fish and served it family-style at the table, along with couscous, and then I walked around with a bowl of the extra oil-garlic-herb marinade to drizzle on each person's fish. Unfortunately, the sauce had separated—the oil floated serenely on top of the sunken chopped herbs; it was not an appetizing look. I approached the table with some trepidation. I figured some guests would be put off by the unattractive oil in the bowl. And I was right. "No, thank you" was the common refrain. I asked one of America's top Moroccan chefs, Mourad Lahlou, for his counsel. The first thing he said was that chermoula always breaks because the ratio of oil to other liquids makes it unstable. In fact, he insisted, in Moroccan cooking, you want the chermoula to break because the separated flavored oil can also be used when you're frying. So my mistake would actually be considered a success in Morocco, a fabulous reminder to open our minds to other ways of cooking and eating.

TOTAL TIME: 30 MINUTES + 30 MINUTES MARINATING   SERVES 8

4 garlic cloves

2 jalapeños, seeded and roughly chopped

2 cups flat-leaf parsley leaves

1 cup cilantro leaves

¼ cup red wine vinegar

1 cup extra-virgin olive oil

1 tablespoon dulce pimentón de la Vera (smoked Spanish paprika)

Small pinch of saffron threads

1 teaspoon kosher salt

½ teaspoon freshly ground black pepper

Two 1-inch-thick 2-pound swordfish steaks, cut into 1-inch cubes

Couscous with Cumin + Carrots (page 213), plain couscous or warm pita bread, diced cucumbers and chopped flat-leaf parsley and mint, for serving

1 Put the garlic and jalapeño in the bowl of a food processor and pulse until finely chopped. Add the parsley and cilantro and pulse until finely chopped. Add the vinegar, olive oil, pimentón, saffron, salt and pepper and process the chermoula until smooth.

2 Reserve half of the chermoula. Pour the remaining chermoula into a large resealable bag and add the swordfish. Rub the chermoula all over the swordfish, seal the bag and refrigerate for 30 minutes.

3 Meanwhile, soak 16 wooden skewers in water, or use metal skewers.

4 Preheat your broiler to high. Line a baking sheet with foil.

5 Remove the swordfish from the bag, allowing the excess marinade to drip off, thread the swordfish cubes onto the skewers and place them on the prepared baking sheet.

6 Broil, turning once, until the kebabs are browned on both sides and firm to the touch, about 3 minutes per side. (Alternatively, grill the skewers in a grill pan or on an outdoor grill until charred in spots and firm to the touch.)

7 Transfer the skewers to a platter and serve immediately, with the reserved chermoula alongside and couscous or warm pita bread, cucumbers, parsley and mint.

MAKE AHEAD The chermoula can be stored in an airtight container in the refrigerator for up to 3 days.

chef tips from **mourad lahlou**

ON THE BENEFIT OF OILY CHERMOULA Chermoula always breaks. There's no other way around it—it's the ratio of oil to other liquids (lemon juice/vinegar/water) that makes it so unstable, especially when subjected to heat. In fact, if a chermoula is any good, it is bound to separate. This is desirable in Moroccan cooking, because the infused oil adds flavor and can also be used to fry foods.

ON MARINATING THE FISH Marinate chunks of swordfish or small, delicate fish (such as dorade or branzino), for 30 minutes or less, or you will only taste the chermoula. For large pieces of fish or whole fish, score the flesh in several places with a knife to allow the marinade to penetrate the fish for up to 2 hours.

WHY DIDN'T I THINK OF THAT?
MORE RECIPE IDEAS FROM MOURAD LAHLOU

- Chermoula's bright, herbaceous flavor makes it an unusual flavoring for condiments such as kimchi, aioli and gremolata.
- Chermoula can also be the base of a consommé for delicate fish or the beginning of a stew, braise or roast.

Mexico City Shrimp

"Rick Bayless is a master at making Mexican recipes accessible to American home cooks, and his recipe for Mexico City Shrimp in a basic *mojo* sauce with lots of garlic, oil and citrus is one of the *Food & Wine* editors' favorites. One Saturday night, I made it with the able assistance of my daughter, Sylvie, and her friends Ale and Christina. We started by roasting the garlic in oil in the oven, but after an eternity, the garlic was still tough and wouldn't smash into a paste. Having learned that giving up too quickly in the kitchen is sometimes my downfall, I just kept smooshing it. But this time, it wasn't me: the garlic was old and dry. Eventually I concluded that I'd done all I could to infuse the oil with garlic flavor, and the girls, now starving, encouraged me to proceed with the recipe. They would have been happy with a straight-on sautéed shrimp with just garlic, lime and chipotle, and this was bound to be better—and it was. When I called Rick to ask him what he would have done in my place, he suggested heating the garlic in the oil at a low temperature on the stovetop to infuse the oil. I far prefer that method, so I've used it here in this slightly tweaked recipe.

TOTAL TIME: 45 MINUTES   SERVES 8 TO 10

12 garlic cloves, crushed
¾ cup olive oil
¼ cup freshly squeezed lime juice
1 canned chipotle chile in adobo sauce, seeded and minced
Kosher salt
3 pounds medium shrimp, shelled and deveined
Freshly ground black pepper
½ cup chopped cilantro
Lime wedges, for serving
Rice, tortillas or corn bread, for serving

1 Put the garlic and olive oil in a small saucepan over low heat and cook, stirring occasionally, until the garlic is softened and just barely starting to brown lightly, 12 to 15 minutes.
2 Remove the saucepan from the heat and use a fork to mash the garlic cloves against the sides and bottom of the pan. Stir the garlic back into the oil, then stir in the lime juice, chipotle and a generous pinch of salt. Transfer the *mojo* to a bowl.

3 Set a large skillet over high heat and add one-third of the *mojo* to it. Heat until the garlic and chipotle begin to sizzle, about 30 seconds. Add one-third of the shrimp and season with a generous pinch of salt and a few grinds of pepper. Cook the shrimp, turning once, until just firm to the touch, bright pink and browned in spots, about 3 minutes. Transfer the shrimp to a platter and repeat the process two more times with the remaining *mojo* and shrimp.

4 Pour whatever *mojo* is left in the pan over the shrimp. Scatter the cilantro on top, surround with lime wedges and serve immediately with rice, tortillas or corn bread.

MAKE AHEAD The *mojo* can be stored in an airtight container in the refrigerator for up to 3 days.

chef tips from **rick bayless**

ON COOKING SHRIMP To make sure the shrimp aren't overcooked, take the pan off the heat just before the shrimp are done. The residual heat will finish cooking them.

ON AN ALTERNATIVE WAY OF MAKING *MOJO* To get even more roasted flavor in the dish, leave the skin on the garlic cloves, lay them in the oil in a large skillet over medium heat and roast, turning regularly, until soft and browned in spots, about 15 minutes. With a slotted spoon, remove the cloves from the oil and let cool until you can peel them; set the oil aside. Peel the garlic, transfer to the bowl of a food processor and pulse until finely chopped. With the machine running, add the oil through the feed tube in a slow, steady stream. Add the lime juice and chipotle and pulse to blend. Then season with salt.

CHEF VARIATIONS
- Make extra *mojo*! It's one of the most versatile seasonings you can have in the refrigerator—spoon it over grilled or roasted vegetables or toss it with pasta, a handful of arugula and a sprinkling of grated Parmesan.
- *Mojo* also takes sandwiches to the next level.

Seared Scallops with Fennel + Citrus Salad

❝ When I first made this easy scallop dish, I channeled my emerging inner chef, not because it was difficult, but because I chose to "supreme" the orange and grapefruit. This is a fancy way of saying that I cut off all of the skin and pith, then cut the segments from the membrane. Usually when I see this step in a recipe, I roll my eyes and move on: it feels like fiddly extra work. But in this recipe, I embrace it, because the rest of the prep is so fast and these juicy wedges, along with the fennel, make the scallops refreshing and a little bit different from the usual.

TOTAL TIME: 30 MINUTES   SERVES 4

1 navel orange

1 grapefruit

1 cup finely diced fennel, plus 2 tablespoons finely chopped fennel fronds

2 tablespoons extra-virgin olive oil

1 teaspoon kosher salt

1 teaspoon freshly ground black pepper

3 tablespoons canola oil

16 sea scallops, tough muscle discarded, patted dry with paper towels

1 Slice the ends off the orange and grapefruit and discard. Working with one fruit at a time, stand the fruit on one end and cut off the rind and white pith, exposing the flesh. Working over a bowl, cut down along both sides of each citrus segment to release it from the membranes, letting the segments drop into the bowl.

2 Add the fennel, fennel fronds, olive oil and ½ teaspoon each of the salt and pepper to the bowl and toss to combine. Set aside.

3 Heat the canola oil in a large heavy skillet over medium-high heat until shimmering. Add the scallops and season with the remaining ½ teaspoon each salt and pepper. Cook until well browned on the bottom, a few minutes at the most, then turn them and cook until well browned on the other side, about another 2 minutes.

4 Transfer the scallops to four plates, spoon over the citrus salad and serve immediately.

Pan-Roasted Lobster with Red Miso + Citrus Sauce

" There is a lot of lobster history in my family. My cooking-adverse mother adores lobster, and surprisingly, even tried to prepare it once or twice. As one story goes, she brought home a bag of the crustaceans and a few got loose and ended up under the radiator; I'm not sure they were ever found. But what I remember best is the time my mother bought lobsters and elected me to put them in the boiling water. I gingerly picked up one specimen and put it in the pot tail first. What came next was not a pretty sight, as its claws desperately stabbed the air above the edge of the pot. I ran out one door and my mother ran out the other; we returned only when the lobster was no longer visible.

When I told seafood genius Eric Ripert of Le Bernardin in New York City that tale recently, he teased me that there would be karmic retribution: I would come back as a lobster in my next life. Eric explained that the most humane way to kill a lobster is to take a sharp knife and sever the spinal cord. The key is first stroking the head of the lobster so that it's calm and not wiggling around, then stabbing it decisively. I tried several times before succeeding. Though I learned how to kill a lobster, I took away an even bigger lesson: the importance of focus. If my mind had been trained on the lobster and only the lobster in that critical moment, I am convinced I would have succeeded with the first cut.

Eric's recipe for pan sautéing lobster here involves much concentration, tenacity and finesse. It is also not for the squeamish! After its swift death, the lobster will keep moving, the tail especially. If all this sounds very daunting, I have a simple solution: substitute shrimp for the lobster and just make the incredibly delicious sauce to serve on top.

TOTAL TIME: 45 MINUTES   SERVES 2

2 small live lobsters (about 1¼ pounds each)
3 tablespoons vegetable oil
Kosher salt and freshly ground black pepper
Red Miso + Citrus Sauce (recipe follows on page 181)

1   Bring a large saucepan of water to a boil over high heat.

2   Meanwhile, place one lobster on a large cutting board and gently rub the top of its head to calm it. Splay its claws, so the head is flat against the board. Hold down the body. Jab a heavy, sharp chef's knife into the head between the eyes, then pull the knife down, as if pulling down a handle, straight through the head. Make sure you have a good grip on your knife by choking up on the handle, and work confidently and swiftly. (The lobster will continue to move but it is no longer alive.)

3   Tuck the tail under the body so you can grab the whole thing in your hand to twist the head off. Lay the lobster tail upside down on the cutting board and cut it lengthwise in half through the softer shell. Then crack it open (almost like opening a book). Remove and discard the intestinal vein that runs down the tail. Repeat with the remaining lobster and refrigerate the lobster tails.

4   Twist off the claws; they should come off easily. Remove the rubber bands. Put the claws in the saucepan of boiling water and cook for 5 minutes, then transfer to a plate to cool.

5   Working with a kitchen towel to protect your hands from the sharp claws, twist the knuckles off the claws. One at a time, place each claw upright on the board, the claw facing the ceiling. Hold the whole claw upright, then tap it against the board to release the meat from the shell. Open the pinchers of the claw and, holding on to the large pincher, give it one authoritative whack between the little spikes of the pinchers with your knife to crack it, then twist the knife gently left and then right to get it out. This will crack the claw in a way that allows you to easily twist the shell and remove the claw in one piece. Use your knife blade to pull the thin layer of white protein away from the surface of the claw and remove the thin cartilage inside of the claw.

6   For the knuckles, lay each one on a kitchen towel, hold it down with one hand and use scissors to cut through the shell. Lay it on the board and use both hands to open the shell if it proves difficult. Use your fingers to remove the meat. Set the claw and knuckle meat aside.

7   Reserve the lobster shells for stock or discard them.

8   Heat the vegetable oil in a large heavy skillet over high heat. Meanwhile, season the lobster tails with salt and pepper. When the oil is shimmering, place the lobster tails flesh side down in the pan, pressing down if they curl up. Once the underside takes on some color, about a

minute or two, carefully flip the tails over and cook until the shells turn bright red and even get slightly charred in spots, another minute or so. Transfer the tails to a cutting board. Put the claw and knuckle meat in the pan, turn off the heat and turn the claws and knuckle once just to warm them on both sides.

9 Meanwhile, insert a fork into the meat in each lobster tail and pull each half out of the shell in one piece. Place the meat back in the pan with the claws and knuckles to warm. (Reserve the shells for stock if you'd like.)

10 Transfer the lobster meat to a paper towel to absorb any excess oil and then arrange on plates. Spoon the sauce around the lobster and serve immediately.

Red Miso + Citrus Sauce

TOTAL TIME: 20 MINUTES   MAKES ½ CUP

1 teaspoon minced shallot
1 teaspoon minced peeled ginger
1 cup freshly squeezed orange juice
1 teaspoon red miso, or to taste
1 tablespoon freshly squeezed lemon juice, or to taste
1 tablespoon freshly squeezed lime juice, or to taste
3 tablespoons extra-virgin olive oil
Kosher salt

1 Put the shallot, ginger and orange juice in a small saucepan over high heat and bring to a boil. Whisk in the miso, turn the heat down to medium-high and boil until the mixture is reduced by half, about 5 minutes.

2 Whisk in the lemon and lime juices and then, whisking vigorously, slowly drizzle in the olive oil until the sauce is thickened and emulsified. Season with salt.

MAKE AHEAD The sauce can be refrigerated for up to 3 days. Rewarm over low heat and season with additional citrus juice or salt if needed.

chef tips from **eric ripert**

ON SHOPPING FOR LOBSTER
Turn the lobster upside down and make sure the underside of the tail, toward the head, is firm and plump. This indicates a fresh, healthy lobster.

ON THE BEST WAY TO KILL A LOBSTER Cutting the spinal cord is the quickest, most humane way. Boiling is a slow process! Start by rubbing the top of the lobster's head to calm it.

ON LOBSTER ANATOMY Long antennae mean the lobster is fresh from the ocean; short ones mean it was kept in a tank. Female lobsters have "hairy legs," and their meat is pinker than the meat of the males. Note the difference between the two parts of the claws—almost like a knife and fork—one is much sharper than the other. One is used for cutting things, the other for grabbing.

ON WHISKING When you whisk a sauce, you must be in control of your whisk. There are three ways of whisking: vigorously side to side (which you want here); making a figure eight; or, when whipping cream in a bowl, making big sweeping motions to incorporate as much air as possible.

ON MAKING A SMOOTH SAUCE For the sauce to emulsify, one liquid (here the citrus juice mixture) must to be boiling and the other (the oil) must not be hot. With the citrus mixture at a boil, whisking continuously, very slowly drizzle in the olive oil until emulsified. Taste for seasoning, adding a bit more salt, lemon, lime or miso if you feel it needs it. The sauce should have lovely, thick volume.

ON FIXING A BROKEN SAUCE
Heat it back up and whisk in more olive oil. Temperature changes can cause a sauce to break.

ON PLATING THE LOBSTER
First transfer the warm meat to a paper towel to absorb any excess oil. Then transfer to the plates. Give the sauce a final whisk and spoon it, choking up on the spoon so you have more control, onto the plates, around but not on top of the lobster. That way, whoever is eating can determine how much sauce is on each piece.

Clams with Garlic, Ginger + Sriracha

❝ Every Saturday, a seafood truck parks about ten minutes from our house in upstate New York. I like to drive up to the truck and scan the handwritten list of daily specials, and then buy all kinds of fish (which my family loves) and shellfish (which my family doesn't love). In order to use the shellfish before it goes bad, I cook it late Sunday night when we get back to Manhattan after the kids have had take-out Vietnamese food. Since I'm the only one eating, I just keep it simple. Sometimes I even just steam the shellfish in water, sometimes it's marginally more elaborate: white wine, garlic, ginger. This is my favorite version of all, which I think would be terrific for a dinner party first course.

TOTAL TIME: 25 MINUTES   SERVES 4 AS A FIRST COURSE

2 tablespoons canola oil
3 tablespoons minced peeled ginger (from a 3-inch-long piece)
4 garlic cloves, minced
3 tablespoons Sriracha
1½ cups white wine (or sake if you have it)
4 dozen littleneck clams, scrubbed
3 tablespoons unsalted butter
3 scallions, thinly sliced

1 Heat the oil in a large heavy pot over medium-high heat until shimmering. Add the ginger and garlic and cook until fragrant, about 15 seconds. Stir in the Sriracha and white wine and bring to a boil over high heat.

2 Add the clams and cover the pot. Let the clams cook until they open, shaking the pot occasionally. Check after 5 minutes and take out the open ones, then continue. Uncover the pot and, using tongs or a slotted spoon, transfer the clams to four serving bowls; discard any that haven't opened.

3 Whisk the butter into the cooking liquid and then pour it over the clams, leaving any grit behind in the pot. Scatter the scallions over the clams and serve immediately.

SERVE WITH Plenty of crusty bread or rice to soak up all of the lovely broth.

Squid with Chorizo + Pickled Jalapeños

" It was a snowy, blustery afternoon in upstate New York and my in-laws, who had been visiting for the weekend, needed to head back home to Maine. They valiantly drove off, only to realize that the roads were too hazardous, so they turned around. We had been planning to eat leftovers and not much more, but with the return of Barclay Sr. and Esther, I stuck my head into the fridge to figure out what I could pull off with my limited stock. I reached for squid, chorizo and pickled peppers—a starting point for a fast Spanish-inspired meal. When everything was prepped, I quickly sautéed the sliced squid—but not quite fast enough. The squid was like little rubber bands in a tasty sauce.

Star chef Michael Chiarello, of the Spanish restaurant Coqueta in San Francisco, had a brilliant tip for the next time I made the dish: "Remember that the squid will carry heat and continue to cook after you take it out of the pan, so look for the squid to be just 50 percent, not 100 percent, opaque."

TOTAL TIME: 15 MINUTES SERVES 4 TO 6

3 tablespoons olive oil
¼ pound Spanish-style dried chorizo, diced (1 cup)
1½ pounds cleaned squid, bodies thinly sliced and tentacles halved, or quartered if large, patted dry with paper towels
Kosher salt and freshly ground black pepper
2 tablespoons finely chopped pickled jalapeños

1 Heat the olive oil in a large heavy skillet over medium-high heat until shimmering. Add the chorizo and cook, stirring, until crispy on the edges, about 2 minutes. Using a slotted spoon, transfer the chorizo to a plate.
2 Turn the heat up to high. Add the squid to the pan, season liberally with salt and pepper and stir-fry until the squid is just 50 percent opaque, about 3 minutes. Transfer the squid to a shallow serving bowl, add the chorizo and jalapeños and toss. Serve immediately.

SERVE WITH Steamed white rice.

WHY DIDN'T I THINK OF THAT?
MORE RECIPE IDEAS FROM MICHAEL CHIARELLO

- Sauté the squid in a very hot pan filmed with olive oil and serve with onion jam. To make the jam, put chopped onions (use several varieties, such as cipollini, scallions, shallots and leeks) and a little minced garlic in a skillet and cover with half an inch of olive oil. Cook over low heat for an hour, then drain the mixture (reserve the oil for another use) and refrigerate for up to a week.

- Put the sliced squid in a baking dish and cover with white wine. Season with salt, pepper and ancho chile and roast in a 350°F oven until tender, about 5 minutes. Strain the sauce into a small pot and set the squid aside. Reduce the sauce, then return the squid to the sauce to warm it. In the summer, toss with arugula and chopped heirloom tomatoes. In the winter, add some white anchovies, fresh bay leaves and chopped rosemary to the cooking liquid.

- For escabeche, prepare the roasted squid as above. Add vinegar to the reduced sauce and mix with sliced onions and pimento peppers. Let cool and serve cold.

- When frying squid, for the crunchiest coating, grind Arborio rice in a spice grinder until it turns to powder. Mix 4 parts rice powder to 1 part all-purpose flour to dredge the squid before frying.

chef tips from
michael chiarello

ON BUYING THE BEST SQUID
Always buy fresh squid; it doesn't freeze well and almost all frozen squid is bleached for color. You'll never make great food from fair ingredients.

ON PREVENTING RUBBERY SQUID To not go over the edge of doneness, remember that the squid will continue to cook after you take it out of the pan.

spiced chickpea + yogurt salad,
page 190

pasta, beans + grains

Spiced Chickpea + Yogurt Salad

" I love feeding my contractor, Jacob. He is the kind of guy who will source a $100 salvage door instead of insisting that his shop make a $1,000 solid-oak one. He's the size of a football player (and, in fact, played a bit in college), so he has an admirable appetite. Recently he offered to make a house call to go over a few small details; I asked him to come at lunchtime. I made a big meal, including these chickpeas flavored with hot oil, inspired by a recipe from Seattle chef Jerry Traunfeld of Poppy. I asked Jacob, a connoisseur of a lot more than generators and vents, what he thought of the chickpea salad. He raised one eyebrow and very delicately inquired about the dressing. He hesitated to say it, but he thought it was too thin. I'd used a local yogurt and it was too watery. Since then, I've made the dish with thicker whole-milk Greek yogurt.

TOTAL TIME: 15 MINUTES   SERVES 8 AS A SIDE DISH

1 cup plain whole-milk Greek yogurt

2 tablespoons freshly squeezed lemon juice

2 teaspoons kosher salt

Three 15-ounce cans chickpeas, drained, rinsed and patted dry with paper towels

1 small fennel bulb, trimmed and finely diced (1½ cups)

½ red onion, finely diced (¾ cup)

3 tablespoons canola oil

½ teaspoon crushed red pepper

1½ teaspoons black mustard seeds

1 teaspoon cumin seeds

1 teaspoon fennel seeds

½ cup finely chopped cilantro

½ cup finely chopped mint

1 Whisk together the yogurt, lemon juice and salt in a large bowl. Stir in the chickpeas, fennel and onion. Set aside.

2 Put the oil in a small skillet set over high heat, add the crushed red pepper and mustard, cumin and fennel seeds and cook, stirring occasionally, until the spices are fragrant and the mustard seeds just begin to pop, about a minute. Pour the hot oil and spices over the chickpeas and stir to combine. Toss with the chopped herbs.

3 Transfer to a serving bowl and serve at room temperature.

MAKE AHEAD The salad can be refrigerated for up to 1 day.

chef tips from **jerry traunfeld**

ON THE POWER OF TEMPERING OIL When you heat spices in oil (called a "tempering oil" in Indian cooking), they become wonderfully toasty and infuse their flavor into the oil, which then carries the essence into the final dish. The tempering-oil technique can be used for dals, curries and rassams (thin Indian soups). There is a similar technique in Chinese cooking called oil-sizzling. Ginger and scallions are scattered over a simply cooked ingredient, like whole fish, and then hot oil is poured over it, followed by soy sauce.

ON OTHER INGREDIENTS TO PUT IN TEMPERING OIL Other ingredients that can impart flavor in a tempering oil are chiles, garlic, ginger and other spices such as cinnamon stick, nigella seeds and cardamom pods. You can even try saffron, thyme, rosemary or sage.

ON PREVENTING BITTER FLAVORS If the spices overcook in the oil, they will turn bitter. By pouring the hot spiced oil over the cool chickpeas, you stop the cooking instantly.

ON BALANCE Balance is one of the most important principles in cooking. In a dish, it's about balance of sweet and sour, salty and bitter, crisp and soft. In a menu, it's about balancing light and rich, spicy and cooling, hot and cold.

Pimento-Cheese Grits

66 One late-summer day, I made a pimento grits side dish with cheddar cheese and a hit of height-of-season fresh corn. I went in search of grits at a country market and choices were limited—so limited, in fact, that I had to substitute polenta for the grits for a kind of Italian-Southern mash-up. Since they're both made from cornmeal, it didn't seem like too big a deal. Until I realized the directions were written in Italian, and the measurements were in grams, not ounces. Since I'm atrocious at math, I asked Barclay, my supersmart husband, to calculate the amount of liquid needed to cook the entire package. Something got lost in translation and when I added the cornmeal to the water, it instantly turned into a brick. I should have just taken a few minutes to consult a conversion chart and calculated the right amount of liquid. Instead, I spent twenty minutes trying to fix a lumpy polenta by adding water.

Southern chef Andrea Reusing, of Lantern in Chapel Hill, North Carolina, had some other suggestions as well. She adds polenta or grits to cold water before turning on the heat to slowly simmer the cornmeal. It is, she promises, a foolproof way of avoiding lumps.

TOTAL TIME: 1 HOUR   SERVES 8 AS A SIDE DISH

4 cups chicken stock or low-sodium chicken broth

2 cups water

Kosher salt

1½ cups coarse yellow or white grits

3 large ears corn, shucked and coarsely grated on a box grater
  (1 cup pulp and juice)

2 ounces cream cheese

1 cup (3 ounces) coarsely shredded cheddar cheese

One 4-ounce jar sliced pimento peppers, drained and chopped

1 Pour the chicken stock and water into a large heavy saucepan and season with a generous pinch of salt. Whisk in the grits, turn the heat to medium-high and bring to a simmer, stirring occasionally with a wooden spoon. Turn the heat to low, place a lid slightly ajar on the saucepan and cook the grits at a low simmer, stirring occasionally, until thickened and tender, about 25 minutes.

2 Add the corn pulp and juice and cook just until the corn has lost its rawness, about a minute.

3 Remove the grits from the heat and stir in the cream cheese, cheddar and pimentos. Season to taste with salt and serve immediately.

chef tips from
andrea reusing

ON PREVENTING SCORCHED GRITS Use a heavy pot and cook the grits over low heat.

ON AVOIDING LUMPS The best way is to add the grits to the pan of cold water and give them a stir, then turn on the heat and bring to a slow simmer, stirring occasionally.

ON PATIENCE The cooking time can be longer than expected—do not serve the grits before they are done.

ON GETTING THE RIGHT CONSISTENCY If your grits get too stiff, whisk in a little hot water a bit at a time. If you add too much liquid, just cook the grits until they thicken (this will be fairly fast over medium-high heat).

ON PIMENTO CHEESE The secret is to add sharp cheddar to the cream cheese along with a little finely grated hard cheese like Parmesan (it gives it another layer of flavor and makes it a little more intense), not too much mayo (Duke's!) and something tangy, like cider vinegar or strong mustard.

ON MAKING GRITS COOK FASTER To speed up the process, soak the grits for several hours, or overnight, in the cooking water.

Minty Quinoa Salad

❝ Quinoa has become one of the most popular foods in America. This leads me to believe, with a rare degree of certainty, that most people don't have a problem cooking it. I don't usually have a problem with it either. But there was that one time. . . . I had forgotten to make a dish for a potluck dinner, so at the last minute, I roughly measured 2 cups of chicken stock into a pan to cook 1 cup of quinoa. The result was soapy and soupy. In my rush, I didn't rinse the quinoa first (rinsing removes the saponin, a natural coating, which can taste soapy) and I didn't measure accurately (that's how it got soupy). I didn't have time to fix it, so I picked up a pie on the way to the supper.

TOTAL TIME: 30 MINUTES   SERVES 8 AS A SIDE DISH

2 cups red quinoa, rinsed well (essential) in a fine-mesh strainer
Kosher salt
¼ cup plus 2 tablespoons freshly squeezed lemon juice
2 garlic cloves, minced
1 teaspoon freshly ground black pepper
⅔ cup extra-virgin olive oil
1 English cucumber, cut into ¼-inch dice (3 cups)
1 bunch radishes, trimmed and cut into ¼-inch dice (1½ cups)
1 large red onion, finely diced (1½ cups)
2 cups roughly chopped flat-leaf parsley
1 cup chopped mint

1 Put the quinoa, 1 teaspoon salt and 3 cups water in a saucepan and bring to a boil, over high heat, then turn the heat down to medium, cover the pan and cook until the quinoa is tender, 12 minutes. Remove the pan from the heat and let it stand, covered, for 5 minutes.

2 Fluff the quinoa with a fork, then spread it out on a baking sheet and let it cool completely.

3 Meanwhile, whisk the lemon juice, 1 teaspoon salt, garlic and pepper together in a large bowl. While whisking, slowly drizzle in the olive oil.

4 Transfer the cooled quinoa to the bowl with the dressing and add the cucumber, radishes, onion, parsley and mint. Stir to combine and season to taste with salt and pepper. Serve at room temperature.

Baked Ziti Arrabbiata

66 The last time I made baked ziti arrabbiata, based on one from the maestro of Italian cooking, Mario Batali, I started cooking early in the afternoon, giving myself ample time to "fail and fix" the dish if necessary.

When I made the béchamel, I thought it was too thin, so I decided to reduce it—but it wouldn't reduce. I assumed my problem was using skim milk (the only milk I had in the house), but my diagnosis was incorrect, as I found out when I told the story to the *Food & Wine* test kitchen crew. They explained that béchamel never, ever gets reduced. If you want a thicker béchamel, you add more flour at the start. I realized I had to stop using my ill-informed instincts to solve a problem.

Mistakes aside, this is my absolute favorite baked pasta, particularly when I'm cooking for a crowd. Mario told me it was one of his favorites, too, so I got a little more advice from him on perfecting it.

ACTIVE TIME: 40 MINUTES   TOTAL TIME: 1 HOUR   SERVES 6 TO 8

¼ cup olive oil, divided, plus more for brushing
1 garlic clove, minced
1½ teaspoons crushed red pepper, divided
One 28-ounce can whole peeled tomatoes, smooshed with your
    hands, juices reserved
Kosher salt
2 tablespoons unsalted butter
2 tablespoons all-purpose flour
2 cups whole milk, warmed
Freshly grated nutmeg
1½ pounds ziti
½ pound mozzarella cheese, cut into ½-inch cubes
1 cup freshly grated Parmesan cheese, divided
1 cup coarse bread crumbs

1 Heat 2 tablespoons of the oil in a medium saucepan over medium-high heat until shimmering. Add the garlic and 1 teaspoon of the crushed red pepper and cook, stirring, until fragrant, just a minute or so. Add the tomatoes, with their juices, and a very large pinch of salt, turn the heat to high and bring the mixture to a boil. Lower the heat

and simmer the sauce until just slightly thickened, about 10 minutes. Set aside to cool.

2 Meanwhile, melt the butter in a medium saucepan over medium heat. Stir in the flour and cook, stirring, until a smooth paste the palest shade of brown forms, about 2 minutes. While whisking continuously, slowly pour in the milk. Bring the sauce to a boil and cook, stirring, until it is nice and thick, about 5 minutes. Turn off the heat and season the béchamel to taste with salt and nutmeg. Set aside.

3 Preheat the oven to 375°F. Brush a 9-by-13-inch baking dish with olive oil.

4 Fill your largest pot with water, bring it to a boil and season liberally with salt. (You might need to cook the pasta in 2 batches, depending on the size of your pot.) Add the ziti and cook it 3 minutes short of the package instructions—you don't want it to cook all the way through, or it will overcook when you bake it. Drain the pasta and transfer it to a large bowl.

5 Add the reserved tomato sauce, the béchamel, mozzarella and ¾ cup of the Parmesan to the ziti and stir well. Transfer the mixture to the prepared baking dish and scatter the remaining ¼ cup Parmesan over the top.

6 Toss the bread crumbs with the remaining 2 tablespoons of olive oil in a small bowl and season with salt. Scatter the bread crumbs over the ziti, then sprinkle with the remaining ½ teaspoon crushed red pepper and a pinch of freshly grated nutmeg.

7 Bake the pasta until it is bubbling and the top is browned, about 15 minutes. Let the pasta rest for 10 minutes before serving.

MAKE AHEAD The dish can be assembled ahead, covered with plastic and refrigerated for up to 2 days. Add an extra 5 to 10 minutes baking time to compensate. You can also bake it, cool it and refrigerate it for up to 1 week, or freeze it for up to 1 month. To reheat the pasta, thaw to room temperature, cover with foil and bake in a 325°F oven until hot all the way through (test with a paring knife or metal skewer).

chef tips from **mario batali**

ON HOW MUCH WATER TO USE FOR COOKING PASTA As much as possible. Imagine that you're dancing and want to be expressive, you need room. The pasta needs room to dance, too. If you're cooking less than 2 pounds of pasta, 8 quarts of water is fine. But you don't need to measure—just use your biggest pot.

ON PRECOOKING PASTA BEFORE BAKING The package tells you exactly how long to cook it. For baked pasta, cook it 3 minutes less than what's called for; it'll be super al dente. Drain it; don't ever rinse it.

ON THE BENEFITS OF BÉCHAMEL When you bake stuff with béchamel, it stays moist and rich. You might ask, "Why not just add cheese?" Cheese breaks! Ricotta in the right hands tends to look wrong. Béchamel, even in the wrong hands, looks right.

ON BÉCHAMEL RATIOS For a light béchamel use a ratio of 1 tablespoon butter to 1 tablespoon flour to 1 cup milk.

ON MAKING BÉCHAMEL Your béchamel will go faster if your milk is warm (you can use the microwave), but don't worry if it's cold. Just take your time! If you add too much milk, just mix some cold butter with flour (this is called *beurre manié*) and whisk it in pinch by pinch until the béchamel thickens. If it starts to boil over, whisk it.

ON OTHER USES FOR BÉCHAMEL Allow it to cool so it gets firmer, then add carbonara ingredients (pancetta, Parmigiano-Reggiano, eggs, black pepper), to make a ravioli filling. Cook the ravioli and toss with butter. All of your pasta fillings will be twice as good if there's some béchamel in them—they will ooze. Béchamel is also great for a croque madame.

ON NUTMEG Nutmeg adds exotic flavor to the béchamel; it takes it to another level.

ON USING CANNED TOMATOES Always use whole tomatoes because then you are in control of the product and know exactly what quality you're getting. Usually canned diced tomatoes are parts of broken whole tomatoes and crushed ones are a mix of all of the leftovers. Crush the tomatoes for the sauce with your hands. The pieces should be the size of your thumb—pieces that are too big don't let you get a bite along with other stuff. Everything should be in harmony.

ON SAUCING BAKED PASTA The most important thing about a pasta dish is the pasta. Dress it like a salad. You don't want to lose the noodles—don't blanket them with cheese.

ON BREAD CRUMBS Cut slices of day-old bread and pulse them in a food processor. For this, I like what we call "fat boy" crumbs. Save finer ones for something like a Milanese.

ON TOPPINGS Sprinkle the Parmesan on top first, before the bread crumbs, so the cheese won't burn. A drizzle of olive oil will help make the crumbs nice and brown. And sprinkle crushed red pepper only on half so if some friends don't want it spicy, they won't go hungry.

ON OVERCOOKED BAKED PASTA If it's overdone, just cut the whole thing into pieces, bread them and fry them!

Fideos with Chorizo + Chipotle

❝ *Fideos* is a dish popular in both Mexican and Spanish cooking in which toasted broken pasta is cooked in a rich, tomatoey sauce. This version is one of my favorites adapted from creative New York City chef Alex Stupak of Empellón Cocina. I decided to make it early one evening with friends who were watching me as I prepped. It may have been the messiest meal I've ever prepared. I did my mise en place neatly: crumbled fresh chorizo, minced garlic and chipotles. Then I broke the angel hair pasta into a pan shimmering with hot butter. That's when I discovered that sticks of dried pasta don't break into 2-inch pieces. They shatter into shards and, like broken glass, go everywhere—on the stovetop, on the floor, on my shoes. But that mistake is easy to fix: just put the pasta in a resealable plastic bag before trying to break it. My second mistake soon became painfully obvious. The pan I'd chosen was too small to hold all of the pasta. So I moved half the pasta bits to the adjacent flat griddle. I looked like a harried short-order cook, moving the pasta around with a spatula in each hand to be sure it toasted evenly. The next time, I made the dish in a large deep skillet that could easily hold all the pasta.

TOTAL TIME: 40 MINUTES   SERVES 6

$^3/_4$ pound angel hair pasta

3 tablespoons unsalted butter

$^3/_4$ pound fresh Mexican chorizo, casing removed, crumbled

3 garlic cloves, minced

1 canned chipotle chile in adobo sauce, seeded and minced, or to taste (add an extra chipotle if you'd like it spicier)

1 cup tomato puree

3 cups chicken stock or low-sodium chicken broth

Kosher salt

Shaved Manchego cheese, cilantro leaves, thinly sliced radishes, sour cream and lime wedges, for serving

1 Put the angel hair in a large resealable plastic bag, seal the bag and break the pasta into 2-inch lengths. (The bag keeps the pasta from flying all over the place.)

2 Heat the butter in a large deep skillet or a large saucepan over medium heat, stirring, until it is fragrant and golden, about 2 minutes. Add the pasta and cook, stirring as best you can, until it's browned all over, about 5 minutes. Transfer the pasta to a bowl.

3 Add the chorizo to the skillet and cook over medium-high heat, breaking up the meat with a wooden spoon, until nicely browned and cooked through, about 5 minutes. Taste the chorizo to see how spicy it is so you can determine how much chipotle you'd like to add. Add the garlic and chipotle and cook, stirring, until fragrant, about 1 minute. Stir in the tomato puree and cook, stirring occasionally, until thickened, about 2 minutes.

4 Add the chicken stock and bring to a boil. Stir in the toasted pasta and simmer, stirring frequently, until the pasta is al dente and coated in a thick sauce, about 5 minutes. Season to taste with salt.

5 Spoon the fideos into shallow bowls. Serve right away, with the cheese, cilantro, radishes, sour cream and lime wedges.

WHY DIDN'T I THINK OF THAT?
MORE RECIPE IDEAS FROM ALEX STUPAK

- To get meaty depth without the chorizo and chicken broth, cook a pot of black beans and use the bean cooking liquid in place of the stock. Serve the fideos with the beans.
- For another vegetarian version, omit the chorizo and sauté, grill or roast mushrooms. They add a ton of umami and a gratifying texture to any dish. Instead of chicken stock, you can use mushroom or vegetable broth or just water.

Fusilli with Spanish Tomato Sauce + Manchego

❝ Marcella Hazan was already a contributor to *Food & Wine* when I got to the magazine. She and her husband, Victor, with whom she did all her work, were imposing figures, prickly perfectionists and absolute geniuses. With only a few ingredients, Marcella could bring the taste of Italy into an American home kitchen. I came to admire both of them enormously, though I was always slightly intimidated. Somewhat paradoxically, I didn't find Marcella's recipes intimidating at all. Her justly famous Butter and Onion Tomato Sauce has only 3 ingredients. That alone was enough reason for me to try it, and it was stupendous. Since I make this dish all the time, I sometimes add my own flourishes. Here's one of my variations.

ACTIVE TIME: 10 MINUTES   TOTAL TIME: 45 MINUTES   SERVES 8

Two 28-ounce cans whole peeled tomatoes
1 small yellow onion, root end trimmed but left intact (so the layers don't separate) and halved lengthwise
2 garlic cloves, lightly crushed
2 teaspoons kosher salt, plus more to taste
2 teaspoons dulce pimentón de la Vera (smoked Spanish paprika)
1½ pounds fusilli
4 tablespoons (½ stick) unsalted butter, cubed
1 tablespoon sherry vinegar
Shredded Manchego cheese, for serving

1 Pour the contents of the tomato cans into a large saucepan and lightly crush the tomatoes with your hands. Stir in the onion halves, garlic, salt and pimentón and bring to a boil over high heat. Then simmer over medium-low heat, stirring occasionally, until the sauce is rich and thick, about 35 minutes.

2 Meanwhile, bring a large pot of salted water to a boil. Add the pasta and cook according to the package directions, timing it so the pasta finishes cooking when the sauce is ready. Drain.

3 Pick out and discard the garlic and onion from the sauce. Stir in the butter and vinegar and season to taste with additional salt. Serve the pasta with the sauce spooned on top and plenty of shredded Manchego.

Vietnamese Rice Noodle + Shrimp Salad

“ My mistake with this dish has nothing to do with cooking and everything to do with parenting. I cook for my family to feed them, yes, but also to bring them into my world, the world of food that I love. For me, every meal is an opportunity for adventure, a discovery, which is why I'm always trying dishes from new cuisines or with ingredients I've never explored before. So for dinner one evening, I picked out a Vietnamese noodle salad from my great friend, fantastic cook and brilliant writer Anya von Bremzen, and simplified it. It's a dish I've eaten and loved in restaurants, including a Thai version at Andy Ricker's Pok Pok in New York City. The noodles are cool and chewy, accented by sprightly mint and crunchy peanuts. My daughter has an excellent palate, and even tweaked a few of the recipes for this book, so I anticipated her loving the dish. Sylvie took one bite and spit it out—the first time I'd seen her do this in her life. The funkiness of the fish sauce got to her. I forgave myself—it's impossible to guess what your kids will like all the time. But, I concluded, it's better to try and spit than to never try at all. The lucky one at this meal was my husband, Barclay, who ate three portions—the two kids' and his own.

TOTAL TIME: 45 MINUTES   SERVES 4 TO 6

1 pound medium shrimp (about 40), shelled and deveined

½ pound thin rice noodles (sometimes labeled rice vermicelli or rice stick vermicelli)

1 green Thai chile or jalapeño, thinly sliced (seeds and all)

2 garlic cloves, roughly chopped

¼ cup sugar

½ cup freshly squeezed lime juice

⅓ cup Asian fish sauce

2 tablespoons boiling water

1 English cucumber, halved lengthwise, seeded and thinly sliced

1 cup mint leaves, roughly chopped

½ cup cilantro leaves, roughly chopped

½ small red onion, thinly sliced

½ cup salted roasted peanuts, roughly chopped

1 Bring a large pot of water to a boil. Add the shrimp and cook until bright pink and firm, 2 to 3 minutes. Using a slotted spoon, transfer the shrimp to a colander and immediately rinse them with cold water. Drain the shrimp well and set aside. Keep the pot of water at a boil.

2 Add the rice noodles to the boiling water and cook until tender, about 4 minutes (taste them to check—the time will vary depending on the brand). Drain the noodles in a colander and immediately rinse them with cold water, then rinse them again with lukewarm water. Using a pair of scissors, in the colander, cut the noodles, so they're not so long. Let the noodles sit for at least 20 minutes.

3 Meanwhile, put the chile, garlic and sugar in the bowl of a food processor and blitz until the mixture looks like green sand. Add the lime juice, fish sauce and the 2 tablespoons of boiling water and process until combined.

4 Toss the noodles and shrimp with the dressing, cucumbers, mint, cilantro and onion in a large bowl. Scatter the peanuts on top and serve.

NOTE The noodles may look and feel tender before they're actually done, but they will still taste like raw rice. The best way to check is to taste them. They seem quite soft by the time you drain them, but after you rinse them, they will firm back up nicely.

MAKE AHEAD The dressing can be refrigerated overnight. Toss with the noodle salad just before serving.

chef tips from **andy ricker**

ON SHOPPING FOR NOODLES
Look for the Vietnamese noodles called *bun,* also known as rice vermicelli or rice stick vermicelli.

ON AN ALTERNATIVE TO RICE VERMICELLI If you want to use bean thread noodles (made of mung bean flour) instead of rice noodles, soak them in warm water until pliable (about 30 minutes), then drop into boiling water for 15 to 20 seconds, drain them well (give the colander a shake) and dress and serve immediately. They're a bit chewier and slipperier than rice noodles, and you should use them right away. Don't let them dry.

ON SALTING THE WATER
Check the package to see if your noodles already have salt in them. If so, there's no need to salt your cooking water. If not, salt the water.

ON COOKING AND DRAINING THE NOODLES Boil the noodles in plenty of water, drain them, rinse them with cold water to stop the cooking and then rinse them with lukewarm water to remove excess starch. Let them sit in the colander for 20 minutes. The noodles hold on to a lot of water and if not drained well, will dilute whatever you're making. When they're a bit drier, they will absorb more

dressing and, therefore, more flavor. This is a good recipe for entertaining— you can cook the noodles, leave them to drain and then dress them at the last minute.

ON CHECKING FOR DONENESS You're not looking for al dente pasta—the noodles should be cooked through, but definitely not be mushy.

ON REHEATING NOODLES If you let them sit for too long and they get cold, heat them in the microwave for 30 seconds.

Gas-Station Fried Rice

66 Roy Choi is a chef I revere. He's honest, creative and humble. And he wants to bring great food to the underserved population of LA, and the kids in the 'hood, not just the fooderati. This philosophy inspired his Kogi trucks there—he could give an average guy a taste of something mind-blowing, like a Korean taco. Roy translated this idea into recipes for the home cook for *Food & Wine* when he made his Gas-Station Tacos—tacos filled with items you can buy on the road. The idea of creating a lot out of a little made a big impression on me, and in homage to Roy, I came up with a meal with beef jerky, eggs, frozen peas, potato chips and leftover rice from a Chinese takeout dinner. The jerky is a terrific substitute for Chinese sausage (and is marginally better for you), and the potato chips are good swaps for the crispy noodles (not so good for you). All told, a very satisfying hack for fried rice, perfect for a beginner cook.

TOTAL TIME: 15 MINUTES   SERVES 4

3 tablespoons canola oil

1 garlic clove, minced

4 scallions, thinly sliced, white and green parts kept separate

Fine salt

4 cups leftover cooked rice, preferably short-grain

2 ounces beef jerky, finely diced (or snipped into small strips with scissors if it's too hard to slice, ½ cup snipped jerky)

½ cup frozen peas, defrosted

4 large eggs, beaten

2 ounces thick kettle-cooked potato chips (2 cups), lightly crushed, plus more for garnish

1 tablespoon soy sauce, plus more for serving

1   Heat the oil in a large nonstick wok or skillet over high heat until shimmering. Add the garlic and scallion whites, season lightly with salt and cook, stirring, until just beginning to soften, about a minute. Add the rice and cook, stirring occasionally, until it's hot and beginning to brown, about 3 minutes. Add the beef jerky and peas and stir to combine.

2   Push the fried rice out toward the edges of the pan to create an empty space in the center. Add the eggs to the center of the pan, season lightly with salt and cook, stirring, until they're just set, 1 to 2 minutes. Stir the eggs into the rice, then stir in the potato chips and soy sauce.

3   Transfer the rice to a serving bowl and sprinkle with the scallion greens and a few more crushed chips. Serve immediately, passing soy sauce at the table.

WHY DIDN'T I THINK OF THAT?
MORE RECIPE IDEAS FROM ROY CHOI

- If you don't have leftover rice, this can be made with noodles. Spaghetti or macaroni—why not?! Another good choice would be orzo.
- Other gas-station ingredients you can toss in to add good cheap flavor include instant ramen flavor packets, hot sauce, ketchup or *chicharronnes* (fried pork rinds).

chef tips from roy choi

ON STIR-FRYING RICE To ensure a great result, use short-grain rice. It's a bit more glutinous than long-grain and retains its moisture even after a day.

ON COOKING RICE FOR FRIED RICE Wash the rice five times before cooking and drain well. Once it is cooked, fluff the rice with a fork, then spread on a baking sheet and cool in the refrigerator, uncovered. The next day, get out a big wok or skillet and go to work.

ON FRYING THE RICE Don't crowd the pan. Make sure to have enough space in your pan so the rice has room to do its thing and crisp up. If not, you will get a sludge of day-old untasty, nasty, ugly warm rice in a pan.

Couscous with Cumin + Carrots

"This dish reflects the end-of-summer bounty—and the power of friendship and chutzpah. My friends John and Mike have a magnificent garden and orchard near our place upstate. They often invite my family over to pick fruit or vegetables. One weekend, when I had to cook for a party and arrived too late for the Amenia greenmarket, I drove up to their house, uninvited, and brazenly asked if they had any vegetables they were willing to share. As always, they were generous—I left with a mound of purple, red and orange carrots and some gigantic yellow pattypan squash. Having this mother lode in hand, I was inspired to make cumin-scented couscous with coriander carrots and squash. I put the cut carrots and squash into the oven at the same time, but the squash slightly overcooked, while the carrots cooked to perfection. Next time, I gave the carrots a five-minute head start. In that time, I diced the summer squash, then popped it into the oven.

ACTIVE TIME: 20 MINUTES   TOTAL TIME: 45 MINUTES
SERVES 8 AS A SIDE DISH

1 pound carrots (6 medium), scrubbed and cut into ½-inch dice
   (2¼ cups)
¼ cup plus 3 tablespoons extra-virgin olive oil
1½ teaspoons ground coriander, divided
¾ teaspoon chipotle powder, divided
Kosher salt
1 pound pattypan squash, yellow squash or zucchini
1 large yellow onion, finely diced (1½ cups)
1 teaspoon ground cumin
2 cups chicken stock or low-sodium chicken broth
2 cups couscous
½ cup cilantro leaves, finely chopped
Lemon wedges, for serving

1 Preheat the oven to 450°F. Line two baking sheets with parchment paper.
2 Put the carrots in a bowl and toss with 2 tablespoons of the olive oil, half of the coriander and chipotle powder and ½ teaspoon salt. Spread the carrots out on one of the baking sheets (set the bowl

aside) and roast, stirring occasionally, until tender and browned, about 30 minutes.

3 Meanwhile, trim the squash and dice it into ½-inch pieces. (You should have about 3¾ cups.) Transfer to the bowl and toss with 2 tablespoons of the olive oil, the remaining coriander and chipotle powder and ½ teaspoon salt. Spread the squash on the second prepared baking sheet and roast until tender and browned, about 25 minutes—or a little less if you're using yellow squash, a little more if you're using pattypan squash.

4 While the vegetables roast, heat the remaining 3 tablespoons of olive oil in a large saucepan over medium-high heat until shimmering. Add the onion, season with 1 teaspoon salt and cook, stirring, until softened, about 5 minutes. Add the cumin and cook, stirring, for 1 minute. Add the chicken stock and bring to a boil, then remove the pan from the heat. Stir in the couscous, cover and let sit for 5 minutes.

5 Uncover the pan and fluff the couscous with a fork, then stir in the roasted vegetables, along with all of their oil. Season with salt.

6 Transfer the couscous to a serving dish and scatter with the cilantro. Serve warm or at room temperature, with the lemon wedges.

MAKE AHEAD The couscous can be refrigerated for up to 4 days. Bring to room temperature before serving.

Cannellini Beans with Fennel + Charred Lemon

> On the photo shoot for this book, I worked with a world-class, globe-trotting food stylist, Susie Theodorou. Susie lives in London and New York City, and her family is Greek. At the end of the project, I asked her for a favorite family recipe, and she gave me one for a dried white beans and lemon dish. It was a perfect parting gift. After ten days of shooting together, Susie was very clear about my capabilities as a cook. The recipe she shared sounded easy and healthy, right up my alley. But, although I soaked the dried beans overnight to be sure they would cook evenly, in the final dish, some were creamy and divine, some were starchy and undercooked. To avoid that the next time, I substituted canned cannellini beans, and I also added chopped raw fennel because, to my taste, the dish needed a little bit of crunch.
>
> If you'd like to make this with dried beans, take the advice of bean evangelist Cesare Casella, of Salumeria Rosi Parmacotto in New York City: Cook your beans in a lot of water at low heat and be sure to taste the beans as you go—and not just one at a time. You have to taste several so that you know if they're cooking evenly. With canned or dried beans the recipe is a lovely evocation of the flavors of Greece.

TOTAL TIME: 15 MINUTES   SERVES 8

¼ cup extra-virgin olive oil, divided, or more to taste

1 small lemon, very thinly sliced, seeds discarded

2 tablespoons freshly squeezed lemon juice, or more to taste

1 large fennel bulb, trimmed and finely diced (2 cups)

¼ cup finely chopped fresh dill

Two 15-ounce cans cannellini beans, drained and rinsed (or 2 cups dried cannellini beans if you want to cook them from scratch; see Chef Tips on page 217)

½ teaspoon kosher salt, or more to taste

Freshly ground black pepper

1 Position the oven rack 6 inches from the heat source and preheat the broiler to high. Line a baking sheet with foil and grease it with 1 tablespoon of the olive oil.

2 Lay the lemon slices in an even layer on the prepared baking sheet. Broil, turning once, until charred in spots, 3 to 5 minutes per side. Transfer the lemon slices to a cutting board and let cool slightly, then chop them as fine as you can—you don't want a mouthful of bitter lemon.

3 Transfer the chopped lemons, as well as the oil from the baking sheet, to a large bowl. Stir in the lemon juice, fennel, dill, beans, salt, pepper and the remaining 3 tablespoons olive oil. Season with more salt, olive oil and/or lemon juice if needed. Serve at room temperature.

NOTES Be sure your broiler is hot before you char the lemon slices. (You can prep the fennel while you wait for it to heat.) If your fennel bulb has its fronds attached, finely chop them and toss them into the salad for another lovely herbaceous note.

MAKE AHEAD The dish can be refrigerated for up to 2 days. Bring to room temperature before serving.

chef tips from **cesare casella**

ON COOKING DRIED BEANS
Make sure you buy good-quality artisanal beans that were harvested the same year (check the package for the date).

- Presoak the beans in warm water for 15 minutes. This will help to remove any dirt that has dried onto the skin. Drain, rinse them thoroughly and rub off any remaining dirt.
- If possible, soak and cook the beans in water with a low pH level (i.e., distilled or spring water), as hard water has a high pH level, which can harden beans.
- Cook beans in a lot of water. As I like to say, they should have enough space to dance.
- Always cook beans over very low heat. You never want your beans to boil—and if they do, they won't necessarily soften and will often break.
- There is no rule for how long to cook beans: you have to continue to taste them to see if they are ready. But don't just taste one bean—taste several so that you can see if they're cooking evenly.
- I cover the beans while they cook to maintain a more even temperature inside the pot. If you prefer to keep the pot uncovered, make sure to stir the beans often.
- Never put anything acidic in the pot with the beans (e.g., tomatoes, vinegar, lemon, wine); the acid will prevent them from softening.
- Many people think that adding salt hardens the beans or prevents them from softening, but that is not true. In fact, you should add some salt to the water when you are soaking your beans as it will help them to expand more gradually. Also season the beans during cooking.

ON STORING DRIED BEANS
Store dried beans in a cool, dark place. If your kitchen is very warm, keep them in the refrigerator or even in the freezer.

ON FREEZING BEANS You can freeze fresh beans, dried beans or cooked beans, but if you freeze cooked beans, freeze them in the cooking water.

ON THE FLAVOR OF BEANS
Beans should taste like beans. Especially when you buy a good-quality bean, you don't want to mask the flavor of the bean itself with too many flavors or ingredients. In Tuscany and throughout Italy, beans are typically served simply dressed with great olive oil and pepper.

Bulgur, Smoked Almond + Cranberry Salad with Tahini Dressing

66 Don't confuse bulgur and buckwheat: Bulgur, a cracked wheat, is a Middle Eastern staple. Buckwheat isn't a wheat at all; it's the grainlike seed of a flowering plant. By mistake, I filled a plastic bag at the "grain bar" at the grocery store with buckwheat instead of bulgur, and I can tell you that the consequences for my salad were pretty dire. Because I was using instructions for bulgur, the buckwheat cooked into an earthy, gummy, brown mess that zoomed me back to the 1970s, when I often accompanied my health-foodie father to "natural" restaurants for lunch. I loved going out with him, but I don't ever need to be reminded of the kasha of my youth. The next time I made this dish, I got the right stuff, bulgur, which I believe has potential to be the new quinoa. It's nutty, chewy, light and fluffy. To make this salad, I took a shortcut and added coarsely chopped smoked almonds to get both a crunchy texture and nutty, smoky flavors from a single ingredient. I also added sweet-tart dried cranberries, a fruit that doesn't need any prep.

ACTIVE TIME: 15 MINUTES   TOTAL TIME: 45 MINUTES
SERVES 8 AS A SIDE DISH

3½ cups chicken stock or low-sodium chicken broth

2 cups coarse bulgur wheat (such as Bob's Red Mill)

Kosher salt

¼ cup tahini

¼ cup plus 2 tablespoons boiling water

¼ cup freshly squeezed lemon juice

2 teaspoons soy sauce

1 tablespoon honey

1 cup smoked almonds, roughly chopped

1 cup dried cranberries

6 scallions, thinly sliced

1 Pour the chicken stock into a medium pot and bring to a boil. Stir in the bulgur, along with ½ teaspoon salt, turn the heat to low, cover and cook until the bulgur is tender, about 15 minutes.

2 Turn off the heat, remove the lid and cover the pot with a clean dish towel. Replace the lid and let the bulgur steam for 10 minutes.

3 Fluff the bulgur with a fork and transfer to a large bowl. Let stand, stirring occasionally, until it stops steaming.

4 Meanwhile, whisk the tahini with the boiling water in a small bowl. Whisk in the lemon juice, soy sauce and honey. Season the dressing to taste with salt.

5 Pour the dressing over the bulgur and toss. Add the almonds, cranberries and scallions and stir to combine. Serve at room temperature.

NOTE To get superfluffy bulgur, ideal for salads, cover the cooked bulgur with a dish towel and then replace the lid after the heat is turned off. The towel absorbs the steam so it doesn't drip back into the pot.

MAKE AHEAD The salad can be refrigerated for up to 3 days. Bring to room temperature before serving.

FAMILY

FRIENDS

granola,
page 222

breakfast, breads + warm toasts

Granola

“ The policy at my kids' schools is that families can give teachers only homemade gifts at the holidays. This is a terrific idea—it creates a personal way to show appreciation to the incredibly important people who shape the children's lives and minds. Many years ago, we chose granola as our family gift. My recipe, modeled after one developed by *F&W*'s longtime recipe goddess Grace Parisi, turned out to be a good option. It was fun to make and was a healthy alternative to the ubiquitous gift of choice, cookies.

The only problem is that, even after years of making it, I still burn the edges on some batches. To salvage the project, I scrape the blackened bits into the "family" container for me, Barclay and the kids and put the beautifully toasty, golden brown granola in containers for the teachers. Looking for a better solution, I reached out to Zoe Nathan, of Huckleberry in Los Angeles. I love her granola and knew she could fix my mistakes. She says the trick is to stir the granola a few times as it's baking and to be sure to rotate the tray to allow for your oven's hot spots.

ACTIVE TIME: 10 MINUTES   TOTAL TIME: 1 HOUR 40 MINUTES + COOLING   MAKES 8 CUPS

¼ cup canola oil

¼ cup pure maple syrup

1 teaspoon pure vanilla extract

1 teaspoon kosher salt

3 cups mixed whole-grain flakes, such as oat, barley, rye and wheat (see Note)

1 cup sliced almonds

2 cups dried fruit (I like a combination of cherries, cranberries and chopped apricots)

2 cups unsweetened puffed rice cereal

1   Preheat the oven to 275°F. Line a baking sheet with parchment paper.

2   Put the oil, maple syrup, vanilla and salt in a large bowl and whisk together. Add the whole-grain flakes and almonds and stir to coat thoroughly.

3 Transfer the mixture to the prepared baking sheet and spread it in an even layer. Bake, stirring occasionally, until dry and golden brown, about 1½ hours; rotate the sheet halfway through baking. Let the granola cool completely.

4 Transfer the granola to a large bowl, and stir in the dried fruit and puffed cereal. Scoop into an airtight container or into jars to give as gifts.

NOTE Bob's Red Mill makes a wonderful 5-Grain Rolled Cereal that works perfectly here. It is widely available in grocery stores, as well as online.

MAKE AHEAD The granola can be stored in an airtight container at room temperature for up to 2 weeks.

chef tips from **zoe nathan**

ON GRANOLA INGREDIENTS Granola is all about having the correct ratio of grains to other stuff. Mine is mostly oats, with the nuts and dried fruit as a complement.

ON GETTING GRANOLA CLUSTERS If you want to make your granola clumpier, it's important that all of your grains are well coated (but be sure not to have excess liquid dripping or pooling on the baking sheet or you won't get clusters).

ON HOW TO AVOID BURNING GRANOLA Bake at a low temperature (275°F is optimal) and stir the granola a couple of times while it's baking. All ovens, even the best ones, have hot spots. So it's very important to rotate the baking sheet (especially if you're super-lazy and don't want to mix the granola).

ON THE WORST GRANOLA MISTAKE Adding the dried fruit before baking the granola. Always add it after the granola is baked and cooled, so it doesn't get dried out and crunchy.

No-Cook Strawberry + Lime Jam

❝ Ellsworth Hill Orchard and Berry Farm in Sharon, Connecticut, has signs along the road for miles in every direction, beckoning people to pick fruit. I always want to go (Farm! Adventure! Food!), but my kids don't see the fun of bending over in the hot sun to pinch berries from seemingly endless rows of small plants. By some miracle, though, one Saturday in June, during the height of strawberry season, they agreed. We picked twelve pounds of fruit (the minimum amount for a substantial discount was ten pounds, and we're overachievers). When we got home, we started making a no-cook strawberry jam inspired by the recipe of *Food & Wine* test kitchen cook Justin Chapple. The simplicity of the recipe charmed me—no need to boil jars, cook fruit or add tons of sugar—until I ended up with strawberry syrup instead of strawberry jam. When a recipe is this simple, the details matter, and I hadn't added enough pectin for the ripe fruit. When I spoke to preservation sorcerer Linton Hopkins, of Restaurant Eugene in Atlanta, he made me feel better about my mistake: "Jam is the craft and art of preserving seasons in a jar," he said. I definitely preserved that bright fruit! The syrup was excellent drizzled over ricotta for dessert, if not so great on toast in the morning.

TOTAL TIME: 30 MINUTES + 1½ HOURS SETTING
MAKES 4 CUPS

1½ cups sugar
¼ cup plus 2 tablespoons Ball RealFruit Instant Pectin
2 pounds strawberries, hulled and quartered (8 cups)
2 packed tablespoons finely grated lime zest (from 4 limes)
¼ cup freshly squeezed lime juice
Kosher salt

1   Whisk the sugar and pectin together in a large bowl.

2   Working in batches, put the strawberries in the bowl of a food processor and pulse until finely chopped. Transfer them to the bowl with the sugar and pectin. Add the lime zest and juice and a pinch of salt and whisk together until the sugar has dissolved.

3   Spoon the strawberry mixture into clean glass jars. Cover and let sit at room temperature until the jam has thickened slightly, about 30 minutes, then refrigerate until the jam has set, about 1 hour, before using.

MAKE AHEAD The jam can be refrigerated for up to 2 weeks.

chef tips from **linton hopkins**

ON THE BEST FRUIT FOR JAM The biggest rookie mistake in jam making is using fruit that's not ripe. It doesn't have to be blemish-free, but it needs to be picked as close to harvest as possible.

ON PECTIN Pectin is a naturally occurring polysaccharide found in fruit such as apples, citrus rinds and berries that acts as a gelling agent. Basically, pectin sets in the presence of heat and items such as sugar, calcium and acid. It sets fruit juices in their starch structure, thereby creating a gel.

ON FRUITS TO AVOID Stay away from starchy fruits such as bananas. Their flavors are better suited to a custard rather than a jam.

ON NEW JAM FLAVORS
- Tomato and cayenne chile jam—I love the play of sweet and heat.
- Black pepper and strawberries, for a great combination of bite and sweetness.
- Coriander and peaches—the dry aromatic blends so well with the peach aroma.
- Tarragon and blackberries—experiment with herbs!

Orange + Raspberry Smoothie

66 My mother rarely cooked. She claims that she made Indian food from time to time, though I don't remember that at all. What I do remember are her blender drinks. She had three favorites: a black-and-white soda (with milk, vanilla ice cream, chocolate syrup and club soda), a vanilla milk shake and "The Special." The Special was a decadent after-school treat made with orange juice and raspberry sorbet. I'd slurp it quickly and get "brain freeze," then recover and slurp some more. Since my mother made these effortlessly, without recipes, I reasoned that I, too, could master blender drinks without help. Happily, I was right. I even riffed here, adding a little Greek yogurt so it's a modern-day tangy, sweet dessert smoothie.

TOTAL TIME: 5 MINUTES   SERVES 1 (EASILY MULTIPLIED)

¼ cup raspberry sorbet, softened
½ cup orange juice
½ tablespoon plain whole-milk Greek yogurt

Put all the ingredients in the blender and puree until smooth. Serve immediately.

Fabulous No-Fail Bran Muffins

" Whenever Tina Ujlaki, the executive food editor of *Food & Wine*, prints out a recipe for me to try at home, she cheerfully marks it up before handing it over, scribbling down shortcuts and other ways to enhance an already great recipe. Adapting is so second nature to Tina that I think she could find an excellent way to rewrite a recipe for steamed milk. One of her favorite recipes is Beth Hensperger's Everyday Maple Bran Muffins, which she made healthier by replacing the butter with canola oil, and they've become one of my favorites, too. A welcome relief from my baking fiascoes, this recipe has yet to trip me up.

ACTIVE TIME: 15 MINUTES   TOTAL TIME: 50 MINUTES + COOLING
MAKES 1 DOZEN MUFFINS

1½ cups buttermilk
2 large eggs
½ cup canola oil
¼ cup pure maple syrup
¼ cup packed light brown sugar
2 cups All-Bran cereal
1 teaspoon baking powder
1 teaspoon baking soda
1 teaspoon fine salt
1 cup all-purpose flour
1 cup chopped dried apricots
¼ cup dried cranberries
½ cup raw sunflower or pumpkin seeds

1 Position a rack in the center of the oven and preheat the oven to 400°F. Line a standard 12-cup muffin tin with paper liners.
2 Whisk together the buttermilk, eggs, oil, maple syrup and brown sugar in a large bowl. Stir in the cereal. Allow the mixture to sit until the cereal is softened. Meanwhile, whisk the flour with the baking powder, baking soda and salt in a medium bowl. Then stir it into the wet ingredients and fold in the dried fruit and seeds, being careful not to overmix the batter.
3 Divide the batter evenly among the prepared muffin cups. Bake until the tops are nicely browned and a toothpick inserted in the center of a muffin comes out clean, about 25 minutes. Allow the muffins to cool completely before serving.

Cacio e Pepe Frittata

66 Never before had I been forced to serve something the texture of a sponge for breakfast, but I had no choice. Inspired by the pasta dish of the same name, I made a cacio e pepe frittata for guests. The frittata had started out promisingly. I beat the eggs enthusiastically, added cheese and pepper, poured it into a cast-iron pan and cooked it briefly on the stove, then put it into the oven, where it puffed up in the most glorious way. But when I cut into it, something was very wrong. Our friends were already at the table, and I'd used up all the eggs in the house. I had to serve them my big failed frittata.

Chef Hugh Acheson believes my mistake was putting the frittata in the oven—it dries out the eggs. "Eggs should never see the oven," he says. With his input, I adapted my recipe so the frittata is cooked in a nonstick pan on the stovetop. It's so much easier this way, and it comes out perfectly every time.

ACTIVE TIME: 10 MINUTES   TOTAL TIME: 30 MINUTES   SERVES 8

12 large eggs
¼ cup half-and-half
½ teaspoon kosher salt
1 tablespoon coarsely ground black pepper, plus more for sprinkling
¼ cup roughly chopped basil (optional)
1 cup (4 ounces) freshly grated Pecorino cheese, plus 2 tablespoons for sprinkling
2 tablespoons unsalted butter

1 Whisk together the eggs, half-and-half, salt and pepper in a bowl. Whisk in the basil if using, and the Pecorino.
2 Melt the butter in a 10-inch nonstick skillet over medium heat. Add the egg mixture and cook, stirring gently with a heatproof spatula, until the edges and bottom just begin to set, about 5 minutes.
3 Sprinkle the top of the frittata with coarsely ground pepper and the remaining 2 tablespoons cheese. Cover the frittata with a lid and cook over medium-low heat, without stirring, until it's set throughout, 12 to 15 minutes. Remove the frittata from the heat, uncover and let it stand for at least 5 minutes before cutting into wedges and serving.

MAKE AHEAD The frittata can be made up to 6 hours in advance and served at room temperature. Leftover frittata can be covered with plastic and refrigerated for up to 3 days; serve cold.

chef tips from
hugh acheson

ON KEEPING YOUR FRITTATA MOIST To avoid a dried-out frittata, never put it in the oven.

ON THE BEST PAN FOR EGGS Eggs love nonstick pans. Keep one just for eggs! And never let the pan rip over heat with nothing in it.

ON CHECKING FOR DONENESS Touch the center: it should be just set. Pull the frittata off the heat right at that moment—remember, it will keep cooking even after you remove it from the stove.

ON MORE GREAT FRITTATA INGREDIENTS Other great frittata ingredients include potato chips, chives and caramelized onions.

Simplest Crepes with Dark Chocolate + Cinnamon

❝ The three most important men in my life have one very unexpected connection: crepes. My father, whom I adored, passed away more than twenty years ago. He was a businessman, an art collector, an architecture buff—one thing he was not was a cook. But on Sunday mornings, he'd sometimes make crepes for us, an act of love. (My mother tells me he fell for crepes on their honeymoon in Nassau, where they ate them almost every day.) It was a very special family ritual.

Fast-forward to today: my husband rarely cooks, but on Sunday mornings, he'll sometimes make crepes, because our son is a picky eater and it's one of the only things he likes for breakfast. Three generations of love united by batter swirled in a pan.

When Barclay isn't around or in the mood to make crepes, I'll step in. Unfortunately, mine don't live up to the legacy of my father's. They are often pocked with flour and a little too thick. So I asked Joanne Chang, of Flour Bakery in Boston, to show me how to avoid these mistakes, and she revealed the secret to making the most miraculously smooth batter ever: mix the warm milk, melted butter and the rest of the ingredients in the blender.

TOTAL TIME: 30 MINUTES   MAKES 18 CREPES

....

½ cup coarsely grated dark chocolate (about 1½ ounces)

¼ teaspoon ground cinnamon

2 tablespoons light brown sugar

4 tablespoons (½ stick) unsalted butter, melted, plus more for cooking

1¾ cups whole milk, warmed in the microwave

4 large eggs

1 teaspoon sugar

2 cups all-purpose flour

¾ teaspoon kosher salt

1 Stir together the chocolate, cinnamon and brown sugar in a small bowl. Set aside.

2 Put the butter, milk, eggs and sugar in a blender and blend until just smooth. Add the flour and salt and blend until the batter is completely smooth.

3 Heat an 8-inch crepe pan or nonstick skillet over medium heat and brush it lightly with melted butter. Pour in ¼ cup batter and, holding the pan by the handle, swirl the pan so that the batter coats the bottom evenly. Cook the crepe until the bottom is just lightly browned, about a minute. Loosen the edges with a spatula, carefully flip the crepe and cook until lightly browned on the other side, about 1 more minute. Transfer the crepe to a platter and roll it up like a loose cigar. Continue cooking and rolling crepes until you've used up all of the batter, brushing the pan with more butter as necessary.

4 Scatter the chocolate mixture over the crepes and serve warm.

MAKE AHEAD The batter can be refrigerated for up to 2 days. Stir well before cooking the crepes.

chef tips from **joanne chang**

ON SUGAR AND EGGS Once you've poured sugar onto eggs, whisk them together immediately. If you leave sugar on top of eggs without whisking them, the sugar will basically cook the egg yolks and cause them to create lumps.

ON PREVENTING CREPES FROM STICKING A nonstick pan is good here! Even so, add butter to the pan every third or fourth crepe.

ON MAKING THIN CREPES Add the batter while holding your pan up on an angle, ladling in just a bit of batter and immediately swirling your pan.

ON CREATING EVEN CREPES Your pan shouldn't be too hot, or the batter will start cooking instantly when it hits the pan and not spread evenly.

Waffles with Apple + Maple Compote

66 My son, William, is a talented sous chef, particularly when applying his prodigious enthusiasm to tasks that require expending a lot of energy, like whipping egg whites. One Sunday morning, we made our own version of Pam Anderson's light yet crispy waffles. I mixed the dry ingredients and handed off the whites to William when I realized I didn't have enough vegetable oil for the recipe. I called my next-door neighbor Alice, who had plenty of vegetable oil to spare. As I went across the hall, William took charge of the stand mixer to turn the liquidy whites to soft peaks. By the time I got back to our apartment, William had whipped right past the firm peaks called for and turned the whites into a substantial mountain range. Not knowing how this mistake would affect the batter, I proceeded with caution, folding in the whites. They didn't incorporate quickly or easily, but they did eventually disappear into the batter.

The result was not what I was expecting: they were the best waffles I'd ever made. For a reality check, I reached out to Tyler Florence, who is the chef at Wayfare Tavern in San Francisco and who is a beacon for breakfast goodness. Before tackling those waffles, I'd made only the kind where I didn't need to whip the eggs because I didn't want to dirty an extra bowl or take the extra time, but now, I'm never going back to quick waffles.

TOTAL TIME: 45 MINUTES   MAKES TWELVE 4-INCH SQUARE
OR EIGHT 6½-INCH ROUND WAFFLES

....

1½ cups all-purpose flour

¼ cup cornstarch

1 teaspoon kosher salt

1 teaspoon baking powder

½ teaspoon baking soda

2 cups buttermilk

¼ cup plus 2 tablespoons vegetable oil, plus more for cooking

2 large eggs, separated

1 teaspoon pure vanilla extract

2 tablespoons sugar

Apple + Maple Compote (recipe follows)

Plain yogurt, for serving

1 Preheat the oven to 200°F.

2 Whisk the flour, cornstarch, salt, baking powder and baking soda together in a large bowl. Whisk in the buttermilk, vegetable oil, egg yolks and vanilla. Set aside.

3 Whisk the egg whites in the bowl of a stand mixer at medium-high speed until they hold soft peaks. Gradually beat in the sugar and then beat until the whites are firm and glossy; do not overbeat. Using a rubber spatula, fold the beaten egg whites into the batter until just incorporated.

4 Preheat your waffle iron and oil it lightly. Cook the waffles according to your machine's directions (I like to fill the iron only in the middle so I end up with what I call waffle fingers). As you cook the waffles, transfer them to a baking sheet in a single layer and keep them warm in the oven.

5 Serve the waffles with the warm compote and yogurt.

Apple + Maple Compote

TOTAL TIME: 25 MINUTES   SERVES 8

....

4 tablespoons (½ stick) unsalted butter
4 apples (Pink Lady, Honeycrisp and Gala work well), cored
    and cut into ½-inch dice
½ teaspoon ground cinnamon
¼ cup pure maple syrup

1 Melt the butter in a large skillet over medium-high heat. Add the apples to the pan, sprinkle with the cinnamon and cook, stirring occasionally, until the apples are softened, beginning to fall apart and heavily caramelized, about 15 minutes.

2 Pour in the maple syrup, stir to combine and cook until the apples are nicely glazed, about 5 minutes. Serve warm.

MAKE AHEAD The compote can be refrigerated for up to 1 week. Rewarm over low heat or in the microwave before serving.

chef tips from **tyler florence**

ON WHIPPING EGG WHITES
There is no way to undo overwhipped egg whites, so pay attention as you go. To check, lift up or hold your whisk perpendicular to the bowl. If the egg whites droop, you have soft peaks. When they slope at a 45-degree angle, you're at medium peaks; if they stick straight out, you have stiff peaks.

ON THE BEST WAFFLE IRON An electric cast-iron Belgian-style waffle maker offers the best of both worlds. The Belgian style has more pronounced grooves, exposing the batter to more surface area as it cooks, resulting in a lighter, crispier waffle.

ON GETTING WAFFLES TO RELEASE EASILY Once cast iron has been properly seasoned, you really don't need a lot of nonstick cooking spray. The oil or melted butter in the waffle batter also helps the waffle release easily.

ON PATIENCE Checking the waffle before the light on the iron goes off never ends well. It takes longer than you might think for waffles to fully cook and become crisp.

ON KEEPING WAFFLES CRISP
Stacking cooked waffles on top of one another on a plate will make them soggy. Instead, keep them warm on a baking sheet in a low oven until you are ready to serve them.

ON HOW TO CLEAN YOUR WAFFLE IRON Use a lightly dampened cloth to wipe the cast-iron cooking surface. After the iron cools down, wipe away any dripped batter or cooking spray on the exterior. If you are using a nonstick surface, don't use metal utensils: they will scrape off the coating.

Baked Muesli with Peach Jam

66 When I have weekend houseguests, I generally let them scavenge in the kitchen for breakfast (a lesson I learned from my husband's fabulous stepmother at the time, who would make a glorious lunch and dinner but allow everyone to fend for themselves for the first meal of the day). Every once in a while, though, I'm motivated to prepare a warm breakfast like this muesli that is also good for snacking. The dish gets oohs and ahhs when I put it on the table. I'm never entirely sure if those are simply sounds of delight or just encouragement to reward me for providing breakfast. Either way, I'm happy to make people happy in the morning.

ACTIVE TIME: 5 MINUTES   TOTAL TIME: 50 MINUTES +
10 MINUTES COOLING   SERVES 8

4 cups of your favorite muesli
2 teaspoons baking powder
½ teaspoon kosher salt
½ cup peach jam
2 cups whole milk
2 tablespoons unsalted butter, melted and cooled
1 large egg
Plain whole-milk Greek yogurt, for serving

1 Preheat the oven to 375°F. Line an 8-inch square baking dish with two long pieces of parchment paper, leaving an overhang on all four sides. This will make it easy to remove the muesli once it's baked.

2 Stir together the muesli, baking powder and salt in a large bowl. Spread half of the mixture in an even layer in the prepared baking dish. Dot the peach jam randomly on top—it's nice to get some bites with jam and others without. Cover the jam layer with the remaining muesli mixture.

3 Whisk together the milk, butter and egg in the same bowl. Drizzle evenly over the muesli mixture.

4 Bake until the top is golden brown and the mixture is quite set, about 45 minutes. Let cool for 10 minutes, then cut the muesli into squares and serve warm with cold yogurt.

MAKE AHEAD The baked muesli can be covered with plastic and refrigerated for up to 3 days. To serve, cut into squares and warm in a 300°F oven for about 10 minutes.

Buttermilk Biscuits with Maple + Black Pepper

> In the morning at our house upstate, I often line up flour, butter, salt and baking powder on the counter so that the kids can come up with "inventions," which means combining those ingredients without a recipe. While they are making up something new, I use the same ingredients but follow a recipe. A favorite is this one for buttermilk biscuits. The kids' "inventions" often come out flat as a puck, somewhere between pancake and scone. And, sadly, even though I follow a recipe, so do mine. I console myself by thinking that I just don't quite have the feel for it.

Confident that with a little help my biscuits could rise above the rest, I consulted Joanne Chang, of Flour Bakery in Boston. She gave me some important pointers, including the terrific advice to fold the dough four times so that the biscuits are tall and have a lot of layers when they go into the oven.

ACTIVE TIME: 15 MINUTES   TOTAL TIME: 35 MINUTES +
(OPTIONAL) 1 HOUR CHILLING   MAKES SIX 3-INCH BISCUITS

....

3 cups all-purpose flour, plus more for your work surface

3 tablespoons sugar

1 tablespoon baking powder

1 teaspoon kosher salt

½ teaspoon baking soda

12 tablespoons (1½ sticks) cold unsalted butter, diced,
    plus more for serving

1¼ cups cold buttermilk

Pure maple syrup, for rubbing the biscuits

Coarsely ground black pepper, for sprinkling

1 Line a baking sheet with parchment paper.

2 Whisk together the flour, sugar, baking powder, salt and baking soda in a large bowl. Using your fingers, work in the butter just until the mixture turns into coarse crumbs with some pea-size pieces of butter remaining. Using a wooden spoon, stir in the buttermilk just until the dry ingredients are evenly moistened.

3 Turn the shaggy dough out onto a very lightly floured work surface and pat it out into a ½-inch-thick rectangle. Fold it in half once and gently pat it so that it's 1 inch thick. Do this three more times, to create layers in the dough. Then roll the dough out to ¾ inch thick with a lightly floured pin: Place the pin in the middle of the dough and roll it forward, then put the pin back in the middle of the dough and roll it backward.

4 Using a lightly floured 3-inch round cutter, stamp out biscuits (in one motion—do not twist the cutter), as close together as possible, and transfer to the prepared baking sheet leaving 2 inches between them. Gently pat the dough scraps together (do not overwork the dough), reroll and cut out more biscuits.

5 If you have time, put the baking sheet in the refrigerator and chill the biscuits for at least an hour before baking—they will be flakier. (If you don't have time, don't worry about this step.)

6 Preheat the oven to 425°F.

7 Use the back of a spoon to rub the biscuits lightly with maple syrup and sprinkle coarse black pepper on top.

8 Place the biscuits in the oven and immediately turn the temperature down to 400°F. Bake the biscuits until they're risen and golden, 15 to 20 minutes. Serve warm, with butter.

VARIATIONS If you prefer sweeter biscuits, skip the pepper topping and just rub them with the maple syrup. Or brush the biscuits with buttermilk instead of maple syrup and sprinkle with sugar or a mixture of three parts light brown sugar and one part ground cinnamon. Or, if you prefer less sweet biscuits, simply brush the tops with buttermilk.

chef tips from joanne chang

ON THE IMPORTANCE OF USING A SCALE FOR MEASURING We've experimented at the bakery and everyone's cup of flour varies (up to 100 grams' difference). So I am very pro-scale. The first question I always ask people when they write to me about their recipes not working is, "Do you have a scale?" Keep in mind that using too much flour will yield leaden biscuits.

ON INCORPORATING BAKING SODA Baking soda can be lumpy, so after you measure it, "grind" it into the flour using your fingertips.

ON WHISKING DRY INGREDIENTS It's important to whisk rather than just stir. It aerates the flour and thoroughly combines the leavening ingredients into the flour.

ON COMBINING BUTTER AND FLOUR Use cold butter. Cut the butter into cubes and chill it. When mixing, you are trying to coat the flour with fat. You want each granule of flour to be protected by the fat so that when you add liquid, the flour has a "buffer" to protect it.

ON MAKING FLUFFY BISCUITS Don't overmix the dough in the bowl—finish it on the floured work surface. A shaggy dough is a good biscuit dough. Turn it out on the board, pat it out into a rectangle, and fold it in half; do a total of four folds. The reason for doing this is that there's water in butter and it will create steam when the biscuits are in the oven, which will create layers—so you want plenty of layers of butter, preferably in flat "flakes." Once the dough is nicely layered, roll it out with a floured pin (the flour will help prevent the dough from sticking to the pin).

ON ROLLING OUT DOUGH When you roll back and forth, you are just pushing the butter back and forth and will end up with overworked dough. Put the pin in the middle of the dough and roll it forward, then pick it up, put it back in the middle and roll it backward.

ON SUGAR Sugar not only makes dough sweet, it also improves the texture. Sugar crystals cut into the butter and aerate it. I always imagine sugar as a million little gardeners cutting into the butter and digging little holes.

ON CUTTING BISCUITS Flour a sharp cutter and then cut the biscuits out as close together as you can—this way you'll have as little dough left over as possible. Don't twist the cutter, just go straight down.

ON THE MOST COMMON MISTAKE Overworking the dough. This usually happens when you overmix the butter into the flour and/or overmix the liquid into the dry mixture in the bowl, instead of finishing the dough on the board.

ON PREVENTING MISTAKES Make sure you aren't missing ingredients. All of our recipes are laminated, and we give everyone dry-erase makers so that they can cross off ingredients as they add them. And tasting along the way is crucial, even in baking!

Date, Almond + Honey Bread

" When I was a kid, I loved Thomas' Date Nut Loaf. It was studded with gooey dates and crunchy walnuts and had a sticky layer on top. I ate it blanketed with cream cheese for breakfast. Ever since Thomas' discontinued it, I'd toyed with the idea of making my own. This is an updated version—closer to a pound cake with fruits and nuts. When I made it recently, though, I was in a hurry and forgot to toss the chopped dates and almonds with flour before mixing them into the creamy batter, so the dates just huddled together, instead of being dispersed throughout the loaf.

I asked the fantastic San Francisco baker Michelle Polzine, of 20th Century Café, for her advice. She agreed that tossing the dates and almonds with flour would have helped, but she also warned against using too much flour, or the dates could have clumps of flour stuck to them. She also recommended sprinkling the dates over the batter, rather than dumping them in all at once, then folding gently to be sure they were distributed evenly.

ACTIVE TIME: 35 MINUTES   TOTAL TIME: 1 HOUR 55 MINUTES +
COOLING   MAKES ONE 10-BY-5-INCH LOAF

½ teaspoon fine salt

½ pound (2 sticks) unsalted butter, at room temperature,
   plus more for the pan

2¼ cups all-purpose flour, divided, plus more for the pan

1½ cups soft pitted dates (about 17 large Medjool dates),
   finely diced

½ cup unsalted roasted almonds, coarsely chopped

2½ teaspoons baking powder

2 ounces cream cheese, at room temperature

¾ cup honey

4 large eggs

1 teaspoon pure vanilla extract

½ teaspoon almond extract

1   Position a rack in the middle of the oven and preheat the oven to 325°F. Butter and flour a 10-by-5-inch loaf pan (see Note); line the bottom with parchment paper and butter the paper.

2   Toss the dates and almonds with ¼ cup of the flour in a medium bowl.

3 Whisk together the remaining 2 cups flour, the baking powder and salt in a large bowl.

4 Put the butter, cream cheese and honey into the bowl of a stand mixer fitted with the paddle attachment, or use a large bowl and a handheld mixer. Beat on medium-high speed until the mixture is very creamy, about 2 minutes. On medium speed, beat in the eggs one at a time, mixing until completely smooth, then beat in the extracts. On low speed, beat in the dry ingredients until just incorporated.

5 Sprinkle the flour-coated dates and almonds over the batter and fold them in until evenly distributed. Transfer the batter to the prepared pan and smooth the top.

6 Put the loaf pan on a heavy baking sheet (to prevent the bottom of the bread from browning too much) and bake for 40 minutes. Then loosely cover the top of the loaf with a piece of foil and bake until the top is browned and a cake tester or skewer inserted in the center comes out clean, another 40 minutes or so (about 1 hour and 20 minutes altogether).

7 Transfer the pan to a cooling rack and allow the loaf to cool to room temperature before slicing and serving.

MAKE AHEAD The cooled loaf can be wrapped in plastic and stored at room temperature for up to 3 days. Leftovers are best sliced, toasted and served with butter.

NOTE Be sure to use a light-colored metal loaf pan or a glass or ceramic pan. The bread takes a while to bake through, and you don't want the bottom and sides to darken too much before it is done.

WHY DIDN'T I THINK OF THAT?
MORE RECIPE IDEAS FROM MICHELLE POLZINE

- Add shredded coconut, ground cardamom, coriander or nutmeg to the batter for a different flavor.

chef tips from michelle polzine

ON PREVENTING CLUMPS OF DATES Toss the dates with a little flour first, but be careful that you don't then have clumps of flour stuck to them. Sprinkle the dates over the batter, rather than dumping them in all at once, and gently fold them in so they are well distributed.

ON KEEPING FRUIT AND NUTS FROM SINKING Large pieces of fruit and nuts are likely to sink to the bottom of the pan—cut them into small pieces.

ON MEASURING Measure liquid ingredients like almond extract over the bottle cap so that if a little spills, you can easily pour it back into the bottle.

ON EVEN BAKING When baking cakes and breads, bake on the center of the middle rack.

ON OVEN TEMPERATURE Opening the oven door too often forces the oven to constantly fire up to maintain temperature, which usually results in a bottom that is quite dark. Good for pie, bad for cake!

Grilled Cheese

❝ Every once in a while, we hold *Top Chef*-style cook-offs at our house upstate. It's kind of goofy but a lot of fun. When Julia Turshen, my collaborator on this book, was visiting, we did The Grilled Cheese Melt-Down. I challenged her to make a better grilled cheese than my own, which is a time-honored kid version. I melted butter in a skillet, placed the cheese between the slices of bread, put the sandwich in the pan and covered it. I love this approach because the bread gets very buttery and toasty as the cheese melts, and it's very easy. Julia chose an entirely different method. She remembered a tip from chef Gabrielle Hamilton, of Prune in New York City, who recommends using mayo instead of butter on the outside of the bread. It's easier to spread and allows you to cover every millimeter of the surface so it can get all crispy. Julia also took an extra step and grated her cheese so it would melt faster and reduce any possibility of burning the bread as it cooked. I hate extra steps, so I scoffed at that. But when her grilled cheese came out browned and crisp and gooey and mine was blackened because the butter in the pan burned, I knew she was the winner of the day.

For further schooling, I consulted the extraordinary baker Chad Robertson, of Tartine Bakery in San Francisco, whose grilled cheese is justly famous. He explained that the moisture in the bread steams as the sandwich cooks, thus helping to melt the cheese. I love knowing this, because now I'll always avoid dry bread for grilled cheese sandwiches.

TOTAL TIME: 10 MINUTES   SERVES 1 (EASILY MULTIPLIED)

2 slices sourdough, white or multigrain bread
1 tablespoon mayonnaise
½ cup coarsely shredded not-too-sharp cheddar cheese

1 Spread one side of each slice of bread with half the mayonnaise, making sure to coat the entire surface. Sandwich the cheese between the bread slices, mayonnaise sides out.

2 Set a cast-iron skillet over medium-low heat and place the sandwich in the skillet. Cook until the underside of the sandwich is gorgeously browned and the cheese is beginning to melt, 3 minutes or so, depending on the thickness of your bread. Carefully flip the sandwich, cover the skillet and cook until the other side is nicely browned and the cheese is completely melted, another 2 to 3 minutes. Cut in half and serve immediately.

chef tips from chad robertson

ON THE ONE-AND-ONLY PAN I always use a well-seasoned, cast-iron skillet. I'm not sure what else I would ever use.

ON IDEAL HEAT If you're using thin slices of bread, cook quickly over high heat. When you're using thicker bread, go long and slow over low heat. Make sure you use enough fat to fry the bread so you achieve maximum contrast between the exterior and the melted cheese interior.

ON THE BEST BREAD FOR GRILLED CHEESE Choose a very moist whole-grain country-style loaf. The moisture in the bread steams internally when you are grilling the sandwich and thoroughly melts the cheese. I typically use a fairly strong cheese, so I like to use a sturdy, full-flavored bread.

ON GETTING GOOEY CHEESE Use a good melting cheese. Some of my favorites are Chimney Rock and Pierce Point from Cowgirl Creamery, along with Gruyère, Comté, Petit Basque and aged cheddars.

ON ADDING FLAVOR Add a layer of sweet or savory jam, such as tomato or onion jam or quince paste.

Four Great Warm Toasts

66 I grew up in the Wonder Bread years, when there wasn't much charm or challenge to making sandwiches. But as the bread culture in America has evolved, so have the possibilities for great sandwiches. Now I use artisan bread and great ingredients, so there is almost no way to fail—unless, of course, something goes awry when I slice it (I always buy whole, uncut loaves so they stay fresh longer). If the bread is too thick, it overwhelms the toppings. If it's too thin, it falls apart. I got some good advice on this from San Francisco's Josey Baker, the Svengali of the slice, who bakes at The Mill. I've also experimented with different breads, including the Indian flatbread naan, which is a great option, since it is delicious warmed to envelop all kinds of ingredients, including melty peanut butter and bursting grapes (and it doesn't even have to be sliced).

Peanut Butter + Grapes on Naan

TOTAL TIME: 5 MINUTES   SERVES 1 (EASILY MULTIPLIED)

Spread creamy peanut butter on warm naan and put some whole red grapes on top. Fold over and eat.

Warm Egg Salad on Sourdough

TOTAL TIME: 15 MINUTES   SERVES 1 (EASILY MULTIPLIED)

Peel 2 hard-boiled eggs as soon as they're cool enough to handle. I like 2 egg whites and just 1 yolk for each sandwich. Very roughly chop the whites and put them in a bowl with the yolk. Add 2 tablespoons of mayonnaise and mash together with a fork, making sure that the egg salad remains chunky. Pile on toasted sourdough bread and season with kosher salt and freshly ground black pepper. Eat it while it's warm. You can also add mustard, chopped celery and/or paprika.

Avocado + Soy Sauce on Whole-Grain Bread

TOTAL TIME: 5 MINUTES   SERVES 1 (EASILY MULTIPLIED)

Slice ripe but firm Hass avocados and lay on toasted whole-grain bread. Drizzle with a few drops of soy sauce and sprinkle with flaky sea salt, such as Maldon.

Goat Cheese, Honey + Walnuts on Multigrain Bread

TOTAL TIME: 5 MINUTES   SERVES 1 (EASILY MULTIPLIED)

Spread a thick layer of fresh goat cheese on toasted multigrain bread. Drizzle with honey and scatter some roughly chopped toasted walnuts on top.

chef tips from **josey baker**

ON BREAD This may seem obvious, but you'll never have exceptional toast if you don't start with exceptional bread.

ON THE THICKNESS OF THE BREAD Dense, hearty breads should be sliced thin, about 1/3 inch; lighter breads can be sliced nice and thick, about 1 inch.

ON TOASTING BREAD Many a slice of toast has not lived up to its potential for lack of time spent in the toaster. Don't be scared: Let that slice get good and toasty, on the cusp of being burnt, to develop an array of delicious flavors and great textures.

ON THE POWER OF BUTTER Any sort of nut butter, fruit spread or other sweet topping tastes even better with a little butter underneath. Don't be shy about covering every inch of the toast with toppings; you want bread and spread in each bite.

Avocado, Tofu + Tomato Breakfast Sandwiches

66 Over the last several years, the breakfast sandwich has emerged as a trendy menu item. Fantastic chefs across the country have figured out how to put an entire meal between two pieces of bread. We've showcased a number of these in the magazine. The pictures always made me hungry—hungry to go out for breakfast! They seemed like too much work to do at home before 8 a.m. But, inspired by the chefs' breakfast creativity, I developed my own very simple recipe.

TOTAL TIME: 15 MINUTES   SERVES 4

2 tablespoons canola oil
Four ¼-inch-thick slices firm tofu, drained and patted dry
    with paper towels
1 tablespoon soy sauce
1 ripe Hass avocado, halved, pitted, peeled and quartered
4 English muffins, split and lightly toasted
1 large ripe tomato, sliced
A few pickles, sliced

1 Heat the oil in a large nonstick skillet over medium-high heat until shimmering. Place the tofu in the pan in a single layer and cook until browned on the underside, about 2 minutes. Carefully flip each piece and cook until browned on the other side, another 2 minutes or so. Drizzle the tofu with the soy sauce, remove from the heat and set the tofu aside (leaving it in the pan will keep it warm while you finish making the sandwiches).

2 Use a fork to mash one avocado quarter into the top half of each English muffin. Layer the tomato slices and pickles on the bottom halves and top each with a slice of tofu. Close the sandwiches with the avocado-slathered top halves and serve immediately.

milk + dark chocolate chip cookies,
page 258

desserts

Milk + Dark Chocolate Chip Cookies

❝ Because I love chocolate chip cookies so much, I have probably made them more than any other food. I was still trying to get them right though, using a recipe based on the famous crispy ones from Tate's Bake Shop. They always came out "cakey" and they often overcooked on the bottom. Advice from passionate amateurs led me to buy new heavy baking sheets for even cooking, as well as a small ice cream scoop to guarantee same-size cookies. But these tips didn't solve all my problems. I needed an expert.

With the assistance of Cheryl Day, of Back in the Day Bakery in Savannah, Georgia, I identified my biggest mistake. I was impatient and didn't bring all of my ingredients to room temperature. "Cold ingredients will not allow a proper mixing, causing many problems in the baking process." That explains why I could never get the butter and sugar to cream properly. With that new information, I tried yet one more time, and to my amazement and delight, got a crispy cookie.

ACTIVE TIME: 35 MINUTES TOTAL TIME: 45 MINUTES + COOLING
MAKES ABOUT 4 DOZEN COOKIES

1 cup unbleached all-purpose flour

1 cup whole wheat flour

1 teaspoon baking soda

$^3/_4$ teaspoon kosher salt

$^1/_2$ pound (2 sticks) unsalted butter, at room temperature

$^3/_4$ cup granulated sugar

$^3/_4$ cup firmly packed dark brown sugar

1 tablespoon milk

1 teaspoon pure vanilla extract

2 large eggs, beaten

6 ounces good-quality milk chocolate, finely chopped (about 1 cup)

7 ounces dark chocolate chips or chucks (about 1 cup)

Maldon or other flaky salt

1 Line two large baking sheets with parchment paper.

2 Whisk together the flours, baking soda and kosher salt in a large bowl. Set aside.

3 Put the butter and granulated sugar in the bowl of a stand mixer fitted with the paddle attachment and beat on medium-high speed until well combined, about 1 minute. (Alternatively, use a handheld mixer and a large bowl.) Add the brown sugar and beat just until creamy, about 1 minute. On medium speed, beat in the milk, vanilla and eggs just until incorporated. Using a rubber spatula, fold in the flour mixture, then fold in both types of chocolate.

4 Using a small (1½-tablespoon) ice cream scoop, drop rounded balls of dough 4 inches apart onto the prepared baking sheets. Refrigerate until the dough is chilled, at least 30 minutes.

5 Position a rack in the middle of the oven and preheat the oven to 350°F.

6 Place one baking sheet in the oven and bake the cookies for 10 minutes. Remove the baking sheet from the oven and sprinkle each cookie with a generous pinch of Maldon salt. Return the cookies to the oven, rotating the baking sheet, and bake for about another 10 minutes, or until the cookies are browned and crisp and smell heavenly. Allow the cookies to cool completely on a cooling rack. Repeat the process with the remaining dough, baking a third and fourth batch of cookies on newly lined sheets after they have cooled.

NOTE These cookies spread a lot even when the dough is cold. Chilling the dough as balls will help the cookies keep their shape. Be sure to leave enough space between the dough balls, or the cookies will run into each other. And let them cool and crisp completely before eating.

MAKE AHEAD The cookies can be stored at room temperature in a cookie tin or jar or another container that isn't airtight for up to 2 days. (An airtight container will make the cookies less crisp.) The dough can be refrigerated in an airtight container, either as one big mass or scooped out into balls, for up to 3 days; the flavors will develop even more. You can bake the cookies straight from the fridge.

chef tips from **cheryl day**

ON THE BEST PANS FOR BAKING Use heavy-weight rimmed aluminum baking sheets, known for their excellent heat conductivity, and line them with parchment paper for a little extra insurance for even baking.

ON CHOCOLATE CHUNKS I like to add chocolate chunks so when you bite into the cookie, you can see big chunks of chocolate.

ON CRISP, BUTTERY COOKIES Don't be afraid to bake cookies for 30 seconds more than specified to add a bit of color to the edges, and for a crisper texture. Color adds depth of flavor.

Super-Fudgy Brownies

66 Brownies are the first recipe I ever conquered. For reasons that I cannot now recollect, at around age ten, I was dispatched to the apartment of a friend of my grandmother's, a master baker, to make brownies. Since then, I've prepared them for parties, for bake sales, for the kids. But recently I baked a batch and, after the first bite, realized I'd done something very wrong. My tongue was assaulted by an overroasted bean flavor. Sometimes you can make mistakes even following recipes you know well. Renato Poliafito and Matt Lewis, who make the most incredible brownies at Baked in Brooklyn, came to my rescue. They surmised that I had burnt the chocolate when I melted it with the butter. Their solution? Melt the chocolate and butter in a stainless steel bowl over barely simmering water, and you'll never have to eat a burnt brownie.

ACTIVE TIME: 15 MINUTES   TOTAL TIME: 50 MINUTES + COOLING
MAKES 1 DOZEN BROWNIES

- ³/₄ cup all-purpose flour
- ¹/₄ cup unsweetened cocoa powder
- ¹/₂ teaspoon kosher salt
- 4 ounces high-quality semisweet chocolate (60 to 70% cacao), finely chopped
- 12 tablespoons (1¹/₂ sticks) unsalted butter, diced
- 1¹/₄ cups sugar
- 3 large eggs, at room temperature
- 1 teaspoon pure vanilla extract
- ¹/₄ cup cocoa nibs (optional)

1 Preheat the oven to 350°F. Line an 8-inch square baking pan with foil or parchment paper, leaving a 2-inch overhang on two opposite sides. This will make it easy to remove the brownies once they're baked.

2 Sift together the flour, cocoa powder and salt into a medium bowl. Whisk well and set aside.

3 Bring a medium saucepan of water to a boil, then turn the heat down to low. Put the chocolate and butter in a medium stainless steel bowl and set it over the pan, being sure not to let the bowl touch the water.

Stir the butter and chocolate together until they're completely melted, 3 to 5 minutes.

4 Remove the bowl from the heat and place it on a kitchen towel to capture any condensation. Whisk in the sugar. Let the chocolate mixture cool slightly, then whisk in the eggs and vanilla until smooth.

5 Use a rubber spatula to fold in the flour mixture. Fold in the cocoa nibs, if you're using them.

6 Transfer the batter to the prepared baking pan. Tap the baking pan on the work surface to release air bubbles. Bake, rotating the baking pan halfway through, until a toothpick inserted in the center comes out with some fudgy crumbs attached (you don't want the toothpick to come out clean—that means you've overbaked your brownies!), 40 to 45 minutes. Remove the pan from the oven and allow the brownie to cool completely on a cooling rack.

7 Lift the slab of brownies out of the pan by the overhanging foil and cut into 12 squares.

MAKE AHEAD The brownies can be wrapped tightly in plastic and stored at room temperature for up to 3 days. Or store them in the refrigerator if you'd like them to be extra fudgy (they get firmer and the flavor deepens).

WHY DIDN'T I THINK OF THAT?
MORE RECIPE IDEAS FROM
RENATO POLIAFITO + MATT LEWIS

- Pour half the brownie batter into the pan, add a layer of salted caramel and then add the remaining batter, so the salted caramel is sandwiched in the middle.
- Add spices, such as cinnamon or ancho chile powder, to the batter.
- Mix warm peanut butter into the melted chocolate.
- Replace the vanilla with maple extract.
- Swirl some pumpkin cheesecake batter into the pan of brownie batter.
- Sprinkle the brownies with sea salt and serve with warm caramel sauce.

chef tips from
renato poliafito + matt lewis

ON MELTING CHOCOLATE AND BUTTER Never melt them in a saucepan directly over heat. They may burn. Melt them in a stainless steel bowl over a pot of hot water. (Don't use glass—even tempered Pyrex can crack.) The water should be just barely simmering—any hotter will create steam, which may seep in and make the chocolate seize (an expensive mistake!). Quickly removed the chocolate and butter mixture from the heat and put a dishcloth under the bowl to capture any condensation so that it doesn't end up in the bowl either.

ON THE BEST CHOCOLATE FOR BROWNIES Use good semisweet chocolate (between 60% and 70% cacao), as brownies are all about the flavor of the chocolate. Make sure there are no extraneous ingredients in the chocolate—read the label. There should only be sugar, cacao and cocoa butter. Soy lecithin is also OK—it's used as an emulsifier.

ON ADDING THE SUGAR TO THE CHOCOLATE Add the sugar to the chocolate-butter mixture when it is still warm, so that the sugar dissolves.

ON MEASURING FLOUR We use a scale in the bakery, but if you don't have a scale, loosen the flour with a spoon in the bag, then lightly spoon it into a measuring cup and sweep it off to level it.

ON THE VALUE OF SIFTING Sifting is important for cocoa powder because it gets lumpy. Sifting guarantees the dry ingredients will be properly distributed.

ON CRACKING EGGS Always break the eggs into a separate bowl before adding them so in the event of a broken shell or bad egg, you won't lose all the other work you've done.

ON THE IMPORTANCE OF ROOM-TEMPERATURE INGREDIENTS Ingredients should be at room temperature: If the eggs are cold and the chocolate is too hot, you will end up with scrambled eggs.

ON THE BEST PAN FOR BROWNIES Bake in a light-colored pan; dark ones will yield overbaked edges. We always line our pans so we can pop the brownies out easily.

ON ELIMINATING AIR POCKETS Before baking, assertively tap the pan on your work surface to remove air bubbles.

ON ADDING TOPPINGS If you add toppings, put them on 10 minutes before you pull out the brownies so they don't burn.

ON TESTING FOR DONENESS Insert a toothpick at a 45-degree angle so you can collect as much stuff on the toothpick as possible; wiggle it around a bit. Roll whatever is on the toothpick between your fingers—if it forms a ball, you know your brownies are done. If it's just wet, they're not done yet.

ON THE DIFFERENCE BETWEEN CHOCOLATE CAKE AND BROWNIES There are two differences: the ratio of flour to wet ingredients (there's less flour in brownies) and the leavening (cakes use baking powder and baking soda, brownies don't). For brownies, eggs are your only leavening agent, so the way you whisk them will determine the texture. A major whisk with lots of air will yield cakelike brownies. Not-so-beaten brownies will be fudgier.

ON LETTING BROWNIES COOL Let them cool completely in the pan before eating: at least a few hours, ideally six. Put the pan on a cooling rack so air can circulate underneath and the brownies cool evenly.

Browned-Butter Banana Squares

66 It is not entirely clear why we always have so many bananas around—my family never seems to eat them at their prime and then we're left with a lot of overripe bananas. That's not the worst thing in the world, since I love banana bread. The problem is that banana bread perfection eludes me. Each time I make it, I'm optimistic. As it bakes, the bread fills the apartment with its glorious aroma, making my expectations rise. I'll usually take a small piece as it cools on the counter and I'm pretty happy. But when I cut into it a few minutes later, the crumb is wet.

When I posed this problem to Hedy Goldsmith of Michael's Genuine Food & Drink in Miami, she asked a question: "Is it possible you added too much banana?" I turned pink. How did she know? And could that really be a problem? I did dump in extra mashed banana, thinking it would add more flavor. But according to Hedy, this makes the banana bread dense. Having solved one mystery, I pushed the recipe further, transforming the bread into a cake with a DIY topping option.

ACTIVE TIME: 30 MINUTES   TOTAL TIME: 1 HOUR + COOLING
MAKES ONE 9-BY-13-INCH PAN (24 SQUARES)

FOR THE CAKE

6 tablespoons (¾ stick) unsalted butter, plus extra for the pan

2 cups all-purpose flour

2 teaspoons baking powder

½ teaspoon baking soda

1 teaspoon kosher salt

1½ cups mashed ripe bananas (about 3 large extremely ripe bananas—the darker the skin, the better)

2 large eggs

½ cup buttermilk

1½ teaspoons pure vanilla extract

¾ cup sugar

1 cup toasted walnuts (see Note), roughly chopped and tossed with 1 tablespoon flour (optional)

FOR THE FROSTING

8 ounces cream cheese, at room temperature

6 tablespoons (¾ stick) unsalted butter, at room temperature

1 teaspoon pure vanilla extract
1 cup confectioners' sugar, sifted

FOR THE TOPPING
1 cup chocolate-covered espresso beans or toasted walnuts
   (see Note), roughly chopped

1 Preheat the oven to 350°F. Line a 9-by-13-inch baking pan with parchment paper, leaving a 2-inch overhang on the long sides. Generously butter the paper and the sides of the pan. Set aside.

2 Put the butter in a small saucepan and cook over medium-high heat until it melts, foams and then, after the foam subsides, turns hazelnut brown. Swirl the pan occasionally while the butter browns. The whole process will take about 5 minutes; be sure to watch carefully, as the butter can go from brown to burnt very quickly. Remove it from the heat and set aside to cool.

3 Whisk the flour with the baking powder, baking soda and salt in a medium bowl. Set aside.

4 Put the mashed bananas in a large bowl and whisk in the eggs, buttermilk, vanilla and sugar. Whisk in the cooled browned butter. Add the dry ingredients and stir with a wooden spoon until the batter just comes together (be careful not to overmix). Fold in the walnuts, if using.

5 Transfer the batter to the prepared baking pan. Bake until the cake is springy to the touch and a toothpick inserted in the center comes out clean, about 30 minutes. Remove the cake from the oven and allow it to cool completely on a cooling rack.

6 For the frosting, put the cream cheese and butter in the bowl of a stand mixer and beat on medium speed until smooth and fluffy, about a minute. (Alternatively, you can do this in a medium bowl with a handheld mixer.) Beat in the vanilla and confectioners' sugar.

7 Spread the frosting all over the cooled cake. Scatter with the chopped chocolate-covered espresso beans or walnuts and cut into two dozen squares. Alternatively, cut the cake into squares, and transfer to plates, set out the bowl of frosting and bowls of toppings and let everyone decorate their own square.

NOTE Spread the walnuts in a pie plate and toast in a 425°F oven, shaking the pan occasionally, until golden and fragrant, about 7 minutes. Transfer to a plate to cool completely.

MAKE AHEAD The frosting can be refrigerated in an airtight container for up to 2 days. Bring to room temperature before frosting the cake.

chef tips from **hedy goldsmith**

ON GETTING THE MOST BANANA FLAVOR Use properly ripe bananas. They should be freckled with brown spots, which indicates that their sugar has come out. Don't skimp on the salt. People are too timid with salt in baking. It's a key ingredient to help boost flavors.

ON THE RIGHT RATIO OF INGREDIENTS To avoid a dense texture, don't put too much mashed banana in the bread, even if you think, "Oh I have an extra ripe banana, why don't I throw it in?" That will create too much moisture and make the banana bread wet.

ON GOOD BAKEWARE I recommend an industrial type of pan—something heavy duty that won't buckle in the heat. Not something from the dollar store. Once you buy a great pan, you will have it for life and can hand it down to your kids with the recipe.

ON KEEPING INGREDIENTS FROM SINKING TO THE BOTTOM Mashing the banana helps it from falling. Don't puree bananas so much that they become liquid. For mix-ins, such as raisins or nuts, toss them with a bit of flour before incorporating them. The flour creates a barrier—a little friction—which helps keep them from sinking.

WHY DIDN'T I THINK OF THAT? MORE RECIPE IDEAS FROM HEDY GOLDSMITH

- The Elvis: Peanut butter + cream cheese frosting with crumbled cooked bacon.
- Spread a thick layer of soft butter on 2 slices of banana bread. Cook them in a panini press until well marked and crispy. Sandwich a scoop of ice cream in between. Voilà! Instant ice cream sandwich.
- Marshmallow Fluff makes a great frosting, especially if it's sprinkled with toasted coconut.

Plum Galette

❝ The last time I made this very forgiving galette, which is based on a Jacques Pépin recipe that appeared in *Food & Wine*, I had a vision. I blitzed the flour and butter in the food processor and quickly squeezed the mixture into a ball. With the dough in a respectable round, I took my lovely old rolling pin, put some flour on it and pressed down on the dough. Instead of rolling out, it rolled up as if it wanted to cuddle with the pin. Taking a disciplinarian's stance, I pushed back to roll out the dough. This time the dough gave way, but a little bit stuck on the pin. And that's when I had the vision: the dough looked like a face that was laughing at me.

My friend Christine was in the kitchen with me, prepping another dish, and I asked for her help. You'll have to toss the dough, I said, and start again. It's a belligerent mess. She looked at me calmly and told me she'd just work with it. No, I insisted, it's really too far gone. She didn't answer. I turned my back and started on slicing the plums. When I looked her way a few minutes later, the dough was perfect. She'd added a little bit of flour and massaged it more, rolled it into a round and was getting ready to put it on a baking sheet to chill in the fridge. So I learned how to make galette dough, but I was also reminded not to make the mistake of giving up.

ACTIVE TIME: 30 MINUTES   TOTAL TIME: 2½ HOURS, PLUS COOLING
SERVES 8

½ cup shelled pistachios

¼ cup plus 3 tablespoons sugar

1½ cups cold all-purpose flour, plus more for rolling

12 tablespoons (1½ sticks) cold unsalted butter, cut into ½-inch pieces

¼ teaspoon fine salt

⅓ cup ice-cold water

¼ cup finely diced crystallized ginger (about 6 slices)

8 large plums (2½ pounds), halved, pitted and cut into ½-inch wedges

2 tablespoons unsalted butter, melted

1 Pulse the pistachios with ¼ cup of the sugar in a food processor, until finely ground. Transfer to a small bowl and set aside.

2 Put the flour in the food processor, add the diced butter and salt and pulse for 5 seconds, or until the mixture resembles coarse crumbs with some chunks of butter still visible. Drizzle the water over the mixture and pulse another couple of times, until large clumps form. Turn the dough out, gather it into a ball and gently press it into a 1-inch-thick disk on a lightly floured work surface.

3 Lightly dust a large piece of parchment paper with flour. Transfer the dough to the parchment and lightly flour the top of the dough. Using a floured rolling pin, roll the dough into a round about 15 inches in diameter and about ⅛ inch thick. The easiest way to roll the dough into an even round is to rotate the dough after each roll. (Move the dough, not your pin!) For a tender, flaky crust, treat the dough gently (pounding it or rolling it hard will result in a tough crust). Transfer the parchment paper with the rolled-out dough onto an upside-down baking sheet. Refrigerate until firm, about 30 minutes.

4 Preheat the oven to 400°F.

5 Stir 3 tablespoons of the crystallized ginger into the pistachio mixture. Spread this mixture evenly over the chilled dough, leaving a 2-inch border. Arrange the plums in concentric circles on top of the pistachio mixture. Sprinkle 2 tablespoons of the sugar and the remaining 1 tablespoon crystallized ginger over the plums. Fold the edges of the dough up over the plums, as if tucking the plums into bed (use the parchment paper to help you do this). If the dough is too cold and firm, wait for a few minutes, until it softens to prevent it from cracking when you fold it.

6 Brush the edges of the dough with the melted butter and sprinkle with the remaining 1 tablespoon sugar.

7 Bake the galette until the crust is nicely browned and the fruit is very soft, about 1 hour. Remove the galette from the oven and let cool in the baking sheet on a rack to room temperature before serving.

NOTE The dough can be refrigerated, well wrapped, for up to 2 days after it's formed into a disk.

chef tips from jacques pépin

ON MAKING THE DOUGH
Make sure that the flour and the butter, especially, are cold. Put the flour in the food processor first and then the butter—if the butter goes in first, it will stick to the bottom of the bowl. The butter is still visible in pieces throughout the mixture after a short blending. The water comes last, and it shouldn't take more than a few seconds for the dough to begin to come together. As soon as the dough comes together, invert it onto the work surface and use your hands to gently push the mixture together into a ball and then into a disk.

ON THE KEY TO FLAKY DOUGH In order for the dough to be flaky, the butter shouldn't be fully incorporated into the dough. If you overwork the dough, the butter will disappear in the flour.

ON ROLLING OUT THE DOUGH If you fool around with the dough too long, the heat of your hands will soften the butter and the dough will stick to your pin. If the dough softens too much, refrigerate it before working with it again.

ON THE IMPORTANCE OF A THINNER DOUGH You will get more flakiness, better browning and baking through with a thinner dough.

Pear + Brown Sugar Upside-Down Cake

> Making caramel—heating water and sugar until you have a golden amber syrup—is a fundamental element of many desserts that I love, none of which I'm predisposed to replicate. I have made mistakes over and over again when I have tried to tackle caramel: I've overcooked it, I've undercooked it and I've ended up with gritty crystallized cooked sugar. Grace Parisi, *Food & Wine*'s longtime recipe goddess, solved the problem with a brilliant shortcut in her recipe for an upside-down apple cake. She got the flavor without actually making caramel by laying the fruit on top of a brown sugar and butter mixture; then she poured over the simple batter. I've adapted her method here with pears instead of apples. Sometimes the best way to solve a problem is to work around it.

ACTIVE TIME: 20 MINUTES   TOTAL TIME: 1 HOUR 15 MINUTES + COOLING   MAKES 8 TO 10 SERVINGS

½ tablespoon unsalted butter, at room temperature, for the pan

FOR THE PEARS

4 tablespoons (½ stick) unsalted butter, at room temperature

½ cup packed dark brown sugar

Pinch of kosher salt

2 ripe but firm pears, such as Bosc or Bartlett, peeled, cored and cut into thin wedges (about ⅓ inch thick)

FOR THE CAKE

2 large eggs

1 cup packed dark brown sugar

⅓ cup whole milk

1 teaspoon pure vanilla extract

1 teaspoon almond extract

12 tablespoons (1½ sticks) unsalted butter, melted and cooled slightly

1½ teaspoons baking powder

½ teaspoon baking soda

1 teaspoon kosher salt

1½ cups all-purpose flour

FOR THE GLAZE

¼ cup confectioners' sugar

1 tablespoon whole milk

¼ teaspoon almond extract

1 Position a rack in the center of the oven and preheat the oven to 350°F. Butter the bottom and sides of a 9-inch round cake pan with the ½ tablespoon butter and line the bottom with a round of parchment paper.

2 For the pears, using a rubber spatula, mash the butter with the dark brown sugar and salt in a large bowl until combined. Using your fingers, spread the mixture evenly in the prepared cake pan. Arrange the pear wedges in the pan in concentric circles (filling in any gaps as necessary with smaller pear wedges).

3 For the cake, whisk together the eggs, brown sugar, milk and extracts in the bowl you used for the butter mixture; whisk in the melted butter. Whisk the flour with the baking powder, baking soda and salt in a medium bowl, then whisk into the wet ingredients until the batter is just smooth. Scrape the batter over the pears and spread it in an even layer, without disturbing the pears.

4 Bake the cake until it is golden and springy to the touch and a toothpick inserted in the center comes out clean, about 55 minutes. Remove the cake from the oven and allow it to cool on a rack for 30 minutes.

5 Run a dinner knife around the inside of the pan to loosen the cake. Place a serving plate over the pan, carefully invert the cake onto the plate and remove the pan. Peel off the parchment paper. Let the cake cool completely.

6 For the glaze, whisk together the confectioners' sugar, milk and almond extract in a small bowl.

7 Drizzle the glaze over the cooled cake. Cut into wedges and serve.

SERVE WITH Crème fraîche.

MAKE AHEAD The cake can be stored in an airtight container at room temperature for up to 2 days.

Challah Bread Pudding with Nutella

66 When I tasted the ice cream bread pudding recipe that Jeni Britton Bauer, of Jeni's Splendid Ice Creams in Columbus, Ohio, created for *Food & Wine*, I was struck by her supersmart shortcut. Instead of making a custard to pour over the bread, she used melted ice cream. When I first made it at home, I ignored the instructions that said to allow the bread to soak in the cream mixture because I didn't have enough time. I just dunked the bread until it was wet and then put the pudding in the oven. Happily, I'd invented my own shortcut. Sometimes a change, even by a not-so-knowledgeable cook, can lead to an improvement. In this case, the pudding took less time and was still delicious. Emboldened, the next time I made the dish, I took another chance: to please my daughter, I swirled in Nutella, a speedy delivery system for chocolate and hazelnut flavor. The pudding was gone with lightning speed.

ACTIVE TIME: 20 MINUTES   TOTAL TIME: 1 HOUR   SERVES 8

1 tablespoon unsalted butter, at room temperature
One 1-pound loaf challah, crusts removed, bread cut into 1-inch cubes (11 cups)
2 pints rich vanilla ice cream (look for a brand with high fat content, preferably Jeni's or Häagen-Dazs), melted, and divided, plus more (optional) for serving
4 large eggs, beaten
½ cup whole milk
1 cup Nutella, divided

1 Position a rack in the middle of the oven and preheat the oven to 350°F. Butter an 8-by-11½-inch baking dish and put the challah in it.

2 Pour 1½ cups of the melted ice cream into a large bowl. Whisk in the eggs, milk and ¼ cup of the Nutella. Pour the mixture over the challah and make sure all the bread is saturated with the custard, stirring gently to soak the bread evenly.

3 Place the dish in the oven and bake until the bread pudding is set (the center should jiggle slightly but not be too wet) and the top is golden brown and puffed, 35 to 40 minutes. Remove from the oven.

4 Heat the remaining ¾ cup Nutella in a small saucepan until it just turns to liquid. Drizzle it over the bread pudding. Serve warm, with additional ice cream if you choose.

Blueberry + Peach Crisp with Graham Cracker Topping

❝ When we were first married, my husband and I would visit his father and then stepmother, Judy, in coastal Maine. Judy is a great cook and a welcoming hostess. When we visited for the weekend, she would effortlessly make dinner for twenty people. I volunteered to make a crisp one day, hoping to be a helpful houseguest. I improvised the graham cracker and oat topping and patted it down over the most beautiful tiny, fresh-picked blueberries and a few glorious peaches. What came out of the oven, though, was not a crisp. The fruit had reduced to almost nothing. It was like a snack bar with a layer of fruit. Even a novice cook like me could identify the problem here! I didn't account for the fruit shrinking during the cooking process.

When I checked in with star baker Sherry Yard, longtime pastry chef for Wolfgang Puck, now at LA's Helms Bakery, she wasn't appalled by my mistake. In fact, she believes in lots of topping. That said, she had other helpful suggestions on improving my crisp, such as adding some nectarines to the peaches and blueberries. "Nectarines are tart and help balance the sweetness of the peaches," she said. Now I've set down the recipe with the right proportions, adding the nectarines, so I never have to wing it again.

ACTIVE TIME: 30 MINUTES   TOTAL TIME: 1¼ HOURS PLUS COOLING
SERVES 8

1 pint (2 cups) blueberries

8 peaches, halved, pitted and sliced into ½-inch wedges

2 nectarines, halved, pitted and sliced into ½-inch wedges

3 tablespoons plus ½ cup packed dark brown sugar

2 tablespoons cornstarch

1 tablespoon freshly squeezed lemon juice

10 graham crackers, crushed into coarse crumbs (2 cups)

1½ cups rolled oats

1 teaspoon fine salt

6 tablespoons (¾ stick) unsalted butter, softened

1 Preheat the oven to 375°F. Line a baking sheet with foil.

2 Put the blueberries, peaches and nectarines in a 9-by-13-inch glass or ceramic baking dish and toss together with the 3 tablespoons brown sugar, the cornstarch and the lemon juice.

3 Combine the graham cracker crumbs, oats, salt, the remaining ½ cup brown sugar and the butter in a medium bowl. Using your fingertips, blend the ingredients to make coarse crumbs.

4 Sprinkle the graham cracker topping evenly over the fruit. Set the baking dish on the prepared baking sheet to catch any drips, and bake the crisp until the top is browned and the filling is bubbling, 45 to 50 minutes.

5 Let the crisp cool for at least half an hour before serving.

SERVE WITH Vanilla ice cream.

MAKE AHEAD The topping can be refrigerated overnight.

WHY DIDN'T I THINK OF THAT?
MORE RECIPE IDEAS FROM SHERRY YARD

- Plum and boysenberry with lime zest. For fun, put finger lime caviar (firm beads from the little citrus called finger limes) on each plate for added pop!
- Crab apple, Pink Lady apple and cranberries, with a whisper of mandarin orange zest.
- Layer raspberries and honey-glazed figs with goat cheese and top with a savory walnut and herb crumble.
- For an unexpected flavor, add ground tea to the topping (jasmine, orange blossom or any floral blend works well) or a splash of Champagne or Prosecco and a bit of honey to the fruit.

chef tips from **sherry yard**

ON CHOOSING THE PERFECT FRUIT Overripe fruit will yield a soft, overly sweet filling, while underripe fruit makes for a tough, crunchy filling.

ON USING A VARIETY OF FRUIT Each kind of fruit brings something to the party. When baking with peaches, add 1 or 2 nectarines, which are firmer and marvelously tart and help balance the peaches.

ON PEACHES Stay away from white peaches for baking—they can be quite delicate unless they are the perfect combination of firm and ripe (which is like the stars aligning).

ON TOPPING TACTICS Lots of topping guarantees continuous crunch: use a high ratio of crumble to fruit. The best crisps also always have a mix of bigger chunks of topping along with smaller pieces. If your crumble begins to brown too much, cover it with foil. Once it's finished baking, immediately remove the foil (you don't want the topping to steam and get soggy).

ON EASY CLEANUP Line a baking sheet with foil and place the crisp on top in case there are renegade bubbling juices.

Coconut Chia Pudding with Mango + Pineapple

66 Chia is a miracle seed and a superfood. I prepped a chia seed pudding one morning to serve my family for dessert and when I went to check on it later, half of it was gone. Its superpower isn't what made it vanish. It was so good that my daughter, Sylvie, and a friend ate it for a snack. Having succeeded once, I made it again, this time adding diced mango and pineapple to the top to make the nutritious dessert a whole lot prettier and even more delicious.

TOTAL TIME: 20 MINUTES + AT LEAST 4 HOURS CHILLING
SERVES 4

1¼ cups chilled coconut milk from the dairy case (not the canned type, which is too viscous)
2 tablespoons pure maple syrup, or more to taste
Pinch of fine salt
¼ cup chia seeds
2 tablespoons heavy cream (optional)
½ mango, peeled and finely diced (about 1 cup)
1 cup finely diced fresh pineapple
Unsweetened shredded coconut, for serving (optional)

1 Whisk together the coconut milk, maple syrup and salt in a large bowl. Whisk in the chia seeds. Let the mixture stand until slightly thickened, about 15 minutes; whisk the mixture a few times while it's thickening to prevent the chia seeds from clumping.

2 Cover the bowl with plastic wrap and refrigerate the pudding until it's nice and cold, at least 4 hours.

3 Whisk the cold pudding. If you'd like it to be extra-creamy, whisk in the optional cream.

4 Divide the pudding among four dessert glasses or bowls and top with the mango and pineapple. Sprinkle with the shredded coconut, if you choose, and serve.

MAKE AHEAD The pudding without the topping can be refrigerated for up to 5 days.

EQUIPMENT PRIMER
13 vital pieces of equipment + how to best use them

1. MICROWAVE

A microwave can be a miracle machine. Used incorrectly, it can easily overcook, overheat and even burn your food. Used correctly, according to your manufacturer's directions, a microwave can save you not only time, but energy too. Some of my favorite uses for the microwave include:

- To open oysters easily, José Andrés advises microwaving them for 5-second intervals until the top shells loosen their grip from the bottom shells.
- To cook crispy bacon without any mess, place 2 layers of paper towels on a microwave-safe plate, lay the bacon on top, without overlapping the slices, and put 2 more layers of paper towels on top. Microwave for 5 minutes.
- For the simplest tomato sauce, toss chopped fresh tomatoes with olive oil, garlic and salt in a microwave-safe bowl and microwave for 30 seconds.
- To soften both the flavor and the texture of minced garlic in a vinaigrette, my friend Wilder advises first microwaving it in olive oil for 30 seconds before proceeding.
- Simple syrup, great for cocktails and more, can be made easily in a microwave: Combine equal parts sugar and water in a microwave-safe bowl and microwave for 1-minute intervals, stirring in between, until the sugar is dissolved.
- To get the most juice from lemons or other citrus fruits, microwave them for 30 seconds before cutting and squeezing them.
- To melt chocolate, put the chopped chocolate in a microwave-safe bowl and microwave it for 30-second intervals, stirring in between, until it's nice and smooth. Remember that chocolate won't visibly melt, so stirring is crucial in order to avoid burning the chocolate.

- If your brown sugar has turned into a brick, put it in a microwave-safe bowl, cover with a damp paper towel and microwave for 20 seconds to help soften it.

Remember:

- Never put metal (including silverware or foil) in the microwave.
- Always stir food and, if the microwave doesn't have a carousel, turn dishes at intervals to make sure things cook evenly.
- Pierce the skins of vegetables such as potatoes and squash before cooking so they don't burst.

2. BLENDER

Blenders are key not only for smoothies and frozen drinks but also for silky soups and creamy dressings. (Though used incorrectly, your dinner can end up splattered all over your kitchen.) If it's within your budget, a Vitamix is an excellent choice. Chefs across the world swear by them.

When blending hot liquids, work cautiously:

- Do not fill the blender more than a third of the way.
- Blend in batches if necessary, to avoid filling the blender too much.
- Put the lid on the blender, remove the center plug and put a kitchen towel on top of the blender in the event any liquid or steam should escape.
- Start on low and slowly work your way up to high to puree ingredients.

A handheld immersion blender is a great and affordable option. Used often in professional kitchens, immersion blenders allow you to blend directly in the pot or bowl without the hassle and mess of transferring ingredients to a blender jar.

When using an immersion blender:

- Always submerge the blender in the food or liquid before turning it on or off.
- Always keep the blade and its hood submerged to avoid splatters.
- Make sure to unplug the blender before cleaning it to avoid injury.

3. FOOD PROCESSOR

While they're similar, food processors accomplish tasks that blenders simply can't (and vice versa). No liquid is needed in order for the machine to do its job, which makes the food processer a great choice for chopping items (e.g., grinding nuts) as opposed to pureeing a creamy soup. In addition to chopping, among other tasks, food processors are great for making pastry dough.

4. BAKING SHEETS

A baking sheet, in my book (literally), means a rimmed pan that measures 18 inches by 13 inches; in professional kitchens, these pans are known as half sheet pans. The best baking sheets are made of thick, durable stainless steel, and the lipped edges prevent foods from slipping off. Baking sheets are essential for baking cookies, roasting vegetables, making granola, toasting nuts and more. They're also great for spreading out cooked grains to cool down quickly.

5. A LARGE HEAVY-BOTTOMED POT

I use this for everything from making stock to braising meat (see the Mushroom + Beef Stew on page 158) to frying pasta for Fideos with Chorizo + Chipotle (page 203). Remember, it's easier to cook a small amount of food in a big pot than a large amount in a small pot!

6. CAST-IRON SKILLET

A cast-iron skillet is one of the most affordable and dependable cooking vessels you can own. It can withstand high temperatures, it retains heat very well and it can even become virtually nonstick with regular use. It's great for everything from frying chicken to cooking eggs to searing a steak. A cast-iron skillet is even great for baking—who doesn't love a skillet of corn bread?

When cooking with cast iron, remember:

- Season your skillet as soon as you get it and repeat the process occasionally (like getting a tune-up for your car). To season the skillet, wash it thoroughly with soap and warm water (it's OK to wash it with soap right before you season it). Dry it thoroughly and then wipe a thin coat of vegetable oil all over the interior and exterior of the skillet. Place the skillet upside down on a rack in a 325°F oven for an hour (put a sheet of foil below the skillet). Then turn off the oven and let the pan cool in the oven.
- Cast iron is a reactive metal. Don't cook highly acidic ingredients like wine, lemon juice or tomatoes in a cast-iron pan, or you run the risk

of damaging the seasoning on the skillet and making your food taste metallic and turn quite dark, even black (see Steak au Poivre, page 145).

- To clean your skillet after cooking, while it's still warm, use just hot water and a stiff brush. If there is food stuck to the pan, scrub it with dampened kosher salt or boil some water in the skillet to loosen it. Do not use harsh scrubbers or soap—both will ruin the seasoned surface. Thoroughly dry the skillet before putting it away to avoid rust.
- If your pan does rust, remove the rust by sprinkling baking soda over the damp pan and scrub it away using a potato that you've cut in half. Rinse the pan and repeat the seasoning process.

7. MICROPLANE GRATERS

These indispensable tools are terrific not only for cheese but also for grating aromatics like garlic, ginger and shallots and for zesting citrus. They're useful for grating chocolate, nuts and whole nutmeg as well.

8. SHARP KNIVES

Nearly every chef I speak to says that there is nothing more important in cooking than having good sharp knives. Having the right tools will always help you prep your ingredients more efficiently.

A few things to keep in mind:

- Eric Ripert recommends always using the right size knives. For example, a paring knife is the best choice for small tasks such as peeling shallots or segmenting citrus fruit (see Seared Scallops with Fennel + Citrus Salad, page 177).
- Eric also says to always have a firm, confident grip.
- Safety first! David Chang recommends keeping your knife at the top of your cutting board when you aren't using it so you don't risk knocking it over onto yourself or anyone else in the kitchen.
- To sharpen your knives, take them to your local hardware or kitchenware store for professional sharpening, then keep them sharp by using a steel. Alternatively, you can use a whetstone or an electric sharpener to sharpen your knives.

9. PARCHMENT PAPER

Parchment paper is indispensable for baking and roasting—it not only makes your baking sheets virtually nonstick, it also makes cleanup easier. (But don't line a baking sheet with it if you're broiling something—it will catch on fire!)

Here are a few other uses for parchment paper:

- As Jean-Georges Vongerichten taught me, it's great for lining your cutting board when slicing beets (see pages 52–53) so that you don't stain your board.
- Susie Theodorou, who styled the photographs in this book, moistens a piece of parchment and places it directly on the surface of meats or chicken when braising them (see the Mushroom + Beef Stew on page 158 and the Braised Chicken with Leeks, Mushrooms + Peas on page 102)—this way, the simmering food doesn't dry out.
- Parchment is wonderful for wrapping up sandwiches and baked goods so you can take them with you or tuck them into a lunch box.

10. YOUR HANDS

Your hands are the most valuable and too-often-underestimated tools in the kitchen. Use them for just about everything—don't be afraid to get in there!

11. SMARTPHONES

Many chefs like Mario Batali use these as timers now. They're also excellent reference tools and cameras, too.

12. DIGITAL SCALE

I've stuck to conventional cup measurements in this book because so many people don't have digital scales in their kitchens, but after talking to lots of chefs and experimenting with using a scale, I'm totally a convert. I now think everyone should use one and measure by weight! You get much more accurate measurements.

13. CAKE TESTER

Many chefs, from Thomas Keller to Kristen Kish, use a cake tester not only for baked goods but also for testing whether proteins like chicken and fish are cooked through. You can buy them at kitchenware stores and restaurant supply stores.

ACKNOWLEDGMENTS

I owe an immeasurable debt of gratitude to an enormous number of people, starting with the extraordinary chefs who taught me cooking lessons and life lessons. They inspire me every day and this project has brought my admiration to a whole new level.

To my divine collaborator, Julia Turshen, for developing the recipes. Her good taste, great spirit and terrific ideas made this an incredibly enjoyable journey.

To Suzanne Gluck for believing that I had a book in me, and to my super-charged agent, Andy McNicol, for her expert shepherding of the concept from idea to reality.

To the team at Ecco, led by Dan Halpern, who must be the smartest, gentlest, most encouraging editor ever. I've admired him since I was twenty-two and can't believe how lucky I am to have worked with such an extraordinary man. Suet Yee Chong for developing the elegant design and bringing out the humor in the layout. Ashley Garland for boosting the book into the world. Judith Sutton for her fabulous copyediting. As well as Craig Young, Eleanor Kriseman and Michael McKenzie.

To the incomparable creative team of photographer John Kernick, assistant Rizwan Alvi, food and prop stylist Susie Theodorou, and her able aides Brett Regot, Laura Kinsey and Bridget Henry Siegel. Jessie Riley for being a hair and makeup magician. And Jim Ludlow of Space28. They all made the shoot a highlight of creating this book.

To Susan Choung for the many, many meticulous and thoughtful reads of the manuscript to ensure its accuracy and consistency. She was my safety net and my sanity.

To the talented testers who cross-checked my recipes: Justin Chapple, Kristin Donnelly and Genevieve Ko. I'm grateful for their diligence and skill.

To Patricia Sanchez for sketching the clever, info-packed template for the pages. To Stephen Scoble and Fredrika Stjarne for their gifted artistic guidance.

To Cheryl Houser whose ceaseless encouragement and storytelling prowess shaped this book. Also, Tina Ujlaki whose culinary spirit imbues every recipe here, as well as at *Food & Wine*. Katie Workman whose copious notes crystallized the book's concept. Mary Ellen Ward, Joan Feeney, Andrew Solomon, John Habich, Barbara Heller, Adina Young, Marcia Ely, Olivia Flatto and Asa Hoffman for constant constructive feedback and continuous cheerleading. Jacqueline Westbrook for being willing to assist with everything and anything, including my bête noire, washing dishes.

To editors and colleagues past and present at *Food & Wine* magazine. I've learned so much from them, including Ed Kelly, Nancy Novogrod, Pam Kaufman, Kate Heddings, Kate Krader, Chris Quinlan, Grace Parisi, Marcia Kiesel, Kay Chun, Rebecca Bauer, Jill Davison and Erika Gable. To the indomitable and inspiring publisher of *Food & Wine*, Christina Grdovic, whose brilliance has made the magazine flourish. As well as to my enthusiastic colleagues at Time Inc, including the ever remarkable Evelyn Webster.

To my upstate posse for their eager offers of help: John Hoffman, Mike McCalman, Christopher Jones, Deborah McAlister Jones, Peg McEnroe, Kieran McEnroe, Andrea Salvatore, Kent Hunter, Jonathan Bee and Christine Anderson.

To all the open-minded eaters who knew they might get a less-than-perfect meal but showed up anyway. You know who you are. Thank you!

To my family: my daughter, Sylvie, who agreed to be my sous chef on many occasions, saving meals from disaster with her keen palate; and to my son, William, whose enthusiasm for dishes he likes is one of the most gratifying things in the world. To my husband, Barclay, for his infinite patience and unconditional support. The one time I know I didn't make a mistake was when I said yes to marrying him.

MY CHEF HERO HONOR ROLLS

I will carry lessons learned from these incredible chefs forever.

Grant Achatz
Alinea, Chicago

Hugh Acheson
Empire State South, Atlanta

José Andrés
Minibar, Washington, DC

Josey Baker
The Mill, San Francisco

Dan Barber
Blue Hill at Stone Barns,
Pocantico Hills, NY

Lidia Bastianich
Felidia, New York City

Mario Batali
Babbo, New York City

Rick Bayless
Frontera Grill, Chicago

John Besh
August, New Orleans

April Bloomfield
The Spotted Pig, New York City

Daniel Boulud
Daniel, New York City

Jeni Britton Bauer
Jeni's Splendid Ice Creams,
Columbus, OH

Sean Brock
Husk, Charleston, SC

Floyd Cardoz
White Street, New York City

Cesare Casella
Salumeria Rosi Parmacotto,
New York City

David Chang
Momofuku Ssäm Bar, New York City

Joanne Chang
Flour Bakery, Boston

Michael Chiarello
Bottega, Yountville, CA

Roy Choi
Kogi BBQ, Los Angeles

Tom Colicchio
Craft, New York City

Cheryl Day
Back in the Day Bakery,
Savannah, GA

Susan Feniger
Border Grill, Los Angeles

Bobby Flay
Gato, New York City

Tyler Florence
Wayfare Tavern, San Francisco

Jose Garces
Amada, Philadelphia

Suzanne Goin
Lucques, Los Angeles

Hedy Goldsmith
Michael's Genuine Food & Drink,
Miami

Alex Guarnaschelli
Butter, New York City

Daniel Holzman
The Meatball Shop, New York City

Linton Hopkins
Restaurant Eugene, Atlanta

Daniel Humm
Eleven Madison Park, New York City

Thomas Keller
The French Laundry, Yountville, CA

Kristen Kish

Mourad Lahlou
Aziza, San Francisco

Edward Lee
610 Magnolia, Louisville, KY

Matt Lewis + **Renato Poliafito**
Baked, Brooklyn, NY

Jenn Louis
Lincoln Restaurant, Portland, OR

Seamus Mullen
Tertulia, New York City

Zoe Nathan
Huckleberry, Los Angeles

Bryant Ng
Cassia, Lost Angeles

Yotam Ottolenghi
Ottolenghi, London

Zak Pelaccio
Fish & Game, Hudson, NY

Jacques Pépin
International Culinary Center,
New York City

Michelle Polzine
20th Century Cafe, San Francisco

Paul Qui
Qui, Austin, TX

Alex Raij
La Vara, Brooklyn, NY

Andrea Reusing
Lantern, Chapel Hill, NC

Andy Ricker
Pok Pok, Portland, OR

Eric Ripert
Le Bernardin, New York City

Chad Robertson
Tartine Bakery, San Francisco

Marcus Samuelsson
Red Rooster, New York City

Nancy Silverton
Osteria Mozza, Los Angeles

Maria Sinskey
Robert Sinskey Vineyards, Napa, CA

Ethan Stowell
Staple and Fancy Mercantile,
Seattle

Alex Stupak
Empellón Cocina, New York City

Michael Symon
Lola Bistro, Cleveland

Jerry Traunfeld
Poppy, Seattle

Ming Tsai
Blue Ginger, Wellesley, MA

Jean-Georges Vongerichten
Jean-Georges, New York City

Alice Waters
Chez Panisse, Berkeley, CA

Jonathan Waxman
Barbuto, New York City

Sherry Yard
Helms Bakery, Los Angeles

Andrew Zimmern
Bizarre Foods with Andrew Zimmern

INDEX

Note: Page references in *italics* indicate recipe photos.